Topics in
Language and Culture
for Teachers

Topics in
Language and Culture
for Teachers

Steven Brown and Jodi Eisterhold

Youngstown State University
and
Georgia State University

Ann Arbor
University of Michigan Press

ISBN 0-472-08916-1
Published in the United States of America by
The University of Michigan Press
Typeset by Sans Serif Inc.
Manufactured in the United States of America

2007   2006   2005   2004   4   3   2   1

Acknowledgments

We received lots of support and help throughout this project. We would like to thank the following individuals: Beth Butters did preliminary research; Luciana Diniz served as a research assistant; Salvatore Attardo, Randall Hogue, and Marc Helgesen read parts of the manuscript; Molly Ludt suggested sources; and Leslie Biaggi answered questions. Special thanks to Christina Bratt Paulston who read the entire manuscript. Kelly Sippell, our editor at the University of Michigan Press, was patient and insightful.

The writing of this book has been generously supported by Youngstown State University in the form of a year's sabbatical awarded to Steve in 2002–2003 and a research assistantship funded in summer 2002 by the Graduate School. Thanks to Provost Tony Atwater and to Dean Peter Kasvinsky. Jodi's work was supported by the Applied Linguistics/ESL Department at Georgia State University, particularly by Gayle Nelson as chair of the department. A special thanks to Jay Eisterhold for the extra doses of love, support, and encouragement that helped see this book to completion.

Grateful acknowledgment is made to the following authors, publishers, and journals for permission to reprint previously published materials.

Allyn and Bacon for Mother and Father images from Tom Humphries, Carol Padden, *Learning American Sign Language*. Published by Allyn and Bacon, Boston, MA. Copyright © 1992 by Pearson Education. Reprint by permission of the publisher.

Brand X Pictures for "Children Sitting on Floor, Studying Globe." Copyright © 2003 Brand X Pictures. All Rights Reserved.

Blackwell Publishing Ltd. for "Kaplan's representation of the development of argument in the essays of different cultures" from "Cultural Thought Patterns in Inter-Cultural Education," from *Language Learning, A Journal of Research in Language Studies,* by Robert Kaplan, Vol. 16, #1, copyright © 1966.

Cambridge University Press for image of "ape symbols" from *The Cambridge Encyclopedia of Language* by David Crystal, copyright © 1987. Reprinted with the permission of Cambridge University Press.

Ben Colman, Larime Photographic, Inc., for image of Asian girl reading newspaper.

Corel for "Villagers." Copyright © 2004 University of Michigan Press and its licensors. All Rights Reserved.

Flat Earth for "Couple outside Department Store Seoul Korea Asia," "Contrasting Pedestrians Japan," "Neon Signs in a Shenzen Street China." Photographs Copyright © 2003 IMS Communications Ltd. www.picture-gallery.com.

Flint Ink and Larime Photographic, Inc. for cover photo of world map in paint.

Fotosearch, LLC/Photodisc (Getty Images) for Upward View of Five Smiling Teens, copyright © 2004.

Gallaudet College Press for images of sign language from *Signs across America*, by Edgar H. Shroyer and Susan P. Shroyer, copyright © 1984.

Library of Congress Prints and Photographs Division, for Helen Keller, LC-USZ62-78999, and Nomadic Kirghiz, Golodnaia Steppe, LC-DIG-prok-11854.

MedioImages for "Man Pointing" image. Reproduced by permission under limited license from Mediocom. Copyright © 2004.

U.S. National Archives & Records Administration (NARA) for image "Training Havasupai Teachers in Reading and Language Instruction Methods, 05/1972."

Contents

Introduction to the Teacher

This book introduces upper-division undergraduates and beginning graduate students to the field of language and culture using sociolinguistic and educational perspectives. It is particularly addressed to pre-school and K–12 (PK–12) teachers in training and is also designed to be used as a reference for practicing teachers. While writing, we tried to make as many links as possible to both students' current lives and their future lives. It was our assumption that our audience was beginning its study of different cultures. Our goal was to get the students to the place where they would go home after class and say, "You know what I learned today?"

The book has 11 chapters, 3 appendices, and a glossary. The first two appendices introduce the students to the family tree of languages and language structure, respectively. The third appendix provides resources for further research and professional development. The glossary is a list of basic, important terms that are also bolded in the text. It serves as a quick reference for review.

In our experience, a course on language and culture can have many different goals and can be taken at many points in the curriculum. This book grew out of a course that has no prerequisite beyond completion of the general-education writing requirement, a course that is one of several PK–12 teachers in training can take to satisfy a requirement for an additional course in linguistics. No linguistic or anthropological background was assumed; the instructor took time to provide background as necessary. This book accordingly makes very minimal assumptions about student knowledge. Some teachers will feel comfortable using the main part of the text only, using the appendices and glossary as necessary for background or review. Others might want to directly teach the first two appendices early on in the course to give a much more formal introduction to linguistics. You know your students and their situation best. This book can be used in either a quarter or semester system.

Each chapter contains:

Before You Read. These questions are designed to get students thinking about issues explored in the upcoming chapter; at least one question is designed for group discussion.

Teaching Scenarios. This section concludes the chapter and highlights the specific issues of greatest relevance to teaching.

Check Your Knowledge. These are literal comprehension questions. This section often includes important words from the chapter to know.

Apply Your Knowledge. Further reading and projects in this section include data gathering and analysis for students.

Reflect. In this section, students are encouraged to make personal connections to the chapter based on their own life experiences.

Expand Your Knowledge. This section includes projects that require out-of-class research. The projects are generally lengthier and may evolve into term papers or class reports.

Suggested Readings. Generally, these readings have not been used as references within the chapter, but are provided to offer a wider perspective on chapter topics. In some cases, these works represent seminal work in the field.

Icons. The following icons appear in the text:
- [🎬] indicates the use of a film
- [🖥] marks an Internet activity
- [🎛] suggests the possibility of group work

A Note about Films

In several places throughout the text, we encourage the use of films. These films can be shown in class or assigned as out-of-class viewing. Films provide students with a look at various cultures that may not be available in the classroom. For a list of films, commercial and noncommercial, we recommend Lee Ziegler's book *Film and Video Resources for International Exchange, Second Edition* (2000, Intercultural Press).

When using films in class, we recommend you watch the film before class and note areas that might intersect with your students' lives. As a pre-viewing activity, ask your students two or three questions to start them thinking about the topic. During in-class viewings, we suggest pausing the film at roughly 15-minute intervals and engaging the students in small-group or whole-class discussions. As a post-viewing activity, you will probably want to connect the film directly to the larger topic you have been discussing in the chapter.

Preliminary Questions

1. What is your family background (on both sides)? Are there any stereotypes associated with these groups? Do you think the stereotypes are true?

2. What groups do you identify with most? Least? Why?

3. ▣▣ Get into groups: Think of a culture or nationality with distinct characteristics. Make a list of these characteristics. What does this group sound like speaking in its own language or in English? What does this group act like in its home culture or in America? Share your ideas with the class. How fair or true are these observations?

Chapter 1 will help you understand the positives and negatives of generalizations that are made in research on language and culture. A positive aspect of generalization is its ability to order data. However, generalizations can turn into stereotypes, and the concepts of deficit theory and ethnocentrism may in turn follow from stereotypes. The power of generalizations will be seen by looking at several models of cultural differences. Finally, we question the role of culture in a globalizing world.

Stereotypes and Generalizations

This is a book about language and its relationship to culture. A book of this kind necessarily makes what are at times broad generalizations about both languages and cultures. Before we begin, we need to ask whether it is correct to do so. There is a fine line between generalizations and stereotypes, with *generalizations* typically being valued more positively. (After all, *Most middle-aged Americans know how to drive* seems fairly innocuous.) *Stereotypes,* on the other hand, are viewed negatively because they are often prejudicial. When does a generalization turn into a stereotype? Can we ever fairly say that all members of a given group think or act in a given way? Probably not. When we make generalizations, we need to automatically qualify the statement with *most* or *often* or similar words. Sociolinguistics, which informs much of the following discussion, studies variety in language use, and we hope you will always keep in mind that variety inherent in *all* groups. The anthropologist Anthony Wallace (1961) said that culture is the organization of diversity. The important thing is not the uniformity of the behavior of members of a given culture but rather the members' "capacity for mutual prediction."

Despite the inherent difficulties in the topic, there have been a number of attempts to explain the differences between people as a function of their languages and cultures. Unfortunately, some of these attempts resort to vague notions like *Confucian society* by which people tend to mean *northeast Asian societies* or *Western individualism* by which people tend to mean *North American and Western European societies*. But are there no differences between Chinese and Japanese culture, or between American and French conceptions of individualism? A moment's thought calls these sorts of categories into question.

Some scholars have, however, attempted to scientifically study differences across cultures. We begin with a brief outline of such studies.

Nisbett and his colleagues (Nisbett et al. 2001; Nisbett 2003) argue that cognitive psychology's assumption that all people share the same mental processes may not be true. They claim that societal differences affect beliefs about the world, including beliefs about the nature of the world and the nature of knowledge. This is so because the way society is organized affects the things people pay attention to. A hierarchical society, for example, sensitizes its members to relationships among things and people, because in these sorts of societies people must be aware of interpersonal connections—who is higher and lower in society. As a result, members of that society may focus on wholes at the expense of parts. To use an old expression, they may see the forest and be unable to see the individual trees.

Social structure may also affect behavior. Nisbett and his colleagues, falling into the trap of categories we have already questioned, say that Westerners, because they grow up in an individualistic society, tend to believe they have control over situations, while Asians, who grow up with more responsibilities to a group, may feel they lack control over their immediate environment. As a result, Asians may explain things in terms of situations while Westerners may explain things in terms of goals.

Before presenting experimental data for these conclusions, Nisbett and his colleagues look historically at Greek and Chinese civilizations, the two ancient civilizations that have most influenced modern cultures (the Greeks influenced Western culture, and the Chinese influenced Asian culture). These researchers present ancient Greek culture as being concerned with logic and argument. Philosophers from the pre-Socratics through Aristotle searched for universal laws of nature. The laws they articulated pointed to an atomistic universe, divided among discrete things with innate properties.

Ancient Chinese civilization, on the other hand, focused on harmony, on dialectic resolution of tensions. It believed the world was continuous, not made of discrete parts. It was difficult for Chinese philosophers to pull the world apart and assign each piece an essence, as the Greeks did. Everything was connected; parts were only pieces of a whole. The difference between the Greeks and Chinese is ascribed to their economies; Greeks were independent hunters, traders, and shepherds, while the Chinese were farmers, dependent on each other for water rights, harvests, and markets.

What is the experimental evidence for these generalizations? What of the hypothesis that Asians see wholes and Westerners parts? In one experiment, the responses of Japanese and Americans to animated scenes of an aquarium were compared. The researchers asked the subjects what they saw. A typical first statement from a Japanese subject commented on the background of the picture while the typical first statement of an American subject commented on the focal fish (the most prominent, central fish). Japanese made significantly more statements about the background, compared to Americans (70 percent more, in fact). When later asked to recognize scenes they had viewed, the Japanese made more errors than the Americans did because they matched the wrong fish to the wrong background. This showed the researchers that the Japanese were seeing the scenes whole, without focusing on individual fish (Nisbet et al. 2001). Further evidence is from Rorschach test responses (inkblot interpretations). Chinese Americans gave more responses involving the whole inkblot card than European Americans did. That is, European Americans focused on one part of the card (Abel and Hsu 1949). Here, we begin to have some problems with the data. It may be useful to compare the cultures of two countries, but does it make sense to compare ethnic groups from the same country and offer cultural explanations for differences? This illustrates the potential danger of this sort of research. How much Chinese culture were these test subjects really aware of? How can we seriously speculate that the responses of Americans with Chinese ancestry are in any way connected with ancient Chinese social organization?

According to Nisbett and his co-researchers, culture also has an effect on explanations people give for why things happen. When asked to speculate on the reasons for mass murders, for example, Americans likely answered that the murderer was probably mentally unstable, while Chinese speculated about the situation that preceded the murder and the societal factors that might have been in play (Morris and Peng 1994; Morris, Nisbett, and Peng 1995).

Researchers have also claimed that culture has an influence on how people categorize. Children were shown three pictures and asked which two went together. When shown a man, woman, and child, Chinese children chose the woman and child as belonging together (as in, the mother cares for the child). American children chose the man and woman (as in, they are both adults). Of a seagull, sky, and dog, Chinese children chose the seagull and the sky (as in, the seagull flies in the sky), while American children chose the seagull and dog (as in, they are both animals). Thus, the groups were operating with different assumptions. The Chinese children adopted a contextual/situational point of view while the American children relied on categories (adults, animals) (Chiu 1972).

This is only a small number of the studies Nisbett and his co-authors survey. Their larger conclusion is that differences in culture and social practices can, and do, lead to differences in thought systems. In this case, these researchers see Asian culture leading to a holistic style of thought and Western culture to an analytical style of thought. While they see the beginnings of the differences in history, they also look at a number of current cultural differences as contributing. Among them, and central to our purposes, is a hypothesis that the differences might be linguistically determined—that is, they might have something to do with differences in language. They point out that many Asian cultures have been influenced by Chinese pictographic characters, which they claim must be understood as wholes. Hence, the holistic style of Asian thought. The alphabet, on the other hand, because it is by its nature atomistic, leads to an analytical style of thought. Differences in grammar between Asian languages and Western languages are pointed out, with Asian sentences supposedly needing more context to be understood. But really, all of this is on rather shaky linguistic turf. Characters can in fact be analyzed as parts (which is the way character dictionaries are organized). The issue of how much context a given language requires to be understood is a complex one.

What is one to finally make of all of this? The attempts to explain differences in cultures have been long lived. What Nesbitt and others working in cognitive psychology have attempted to do is interesting because they have sought to collect data in controlled environments. Unfortunately, they often wind up making some unwarranted claims. We have presented their findings as a way to address the issue of generalizations and stereotypes; we hope that reading about this research has stimulated you to think beyond a knee-jerk reaction. To close this section, we will point out that Nesbitt's focus on culture as social practice links his work with the work of some of the people we will be discussing in the next chapter, people who look at what is called *situated cognition*.

Deficit Theories

Differences between cultures have historically been perceived by those in power, and sometimes by those out of power who have adopted the views of the dominant group, as *deficits*: because people are different, they are inferior. This is true not only of culture but also of language; children who go to U.S. schools speaking stigmatized dialects such as African-American English have frequently been branded as cognitively deficient (Morgan 2002). This has also been true of children speaking other languages. When students are different from those in the dominant group, they are often perceived as lacking in skills, preparation, intelligence, or some other quality. This has been called the **deficit model**. Of course, this is ridiculous. Saying that people differ implies no valuable judgment, or it should not. Saying that people who are different are inferior is a form of **ethnocentrism**, the view that one's own culture is the only way to be and is therefore superior. The Conference on College Composition and Communication's 1974 resolution "Students' Right to Their Own Language" explicitly denounced the valuing of one dialect over another and called for teachers to be educated to respect linguistic diversity. It has revisited and reaffirmed its support for linguistic diversity several times in the intervening years (Parks 2000). The Oakland Ebonics controversy, which we will visit in Chapter 8, resulted in the Linguistic Society of America similarly recognizing the legitimacy of all varieties of a given language (Baugh 2000).

Distinguishing Cultures

Dichotomous models, which distinguish two groups based on an opposition or difference between them, are as old as the oldest social science. Sociologists have often divided societies into two types like urban/rural and feudalistic/capitalistic. One important model in early sociology was Ferdinand Tonnies's pair

Gemeinschaft und Gesellschaft. The former term labeled the old community-based society that Tonnies saw fading away in 1887, at the time he was writing. The latter was a label for the emerging modern, rational society based on contracts. Tonnies saw many of the problems of his time as coming from the disjunctions that occurred as the move was made from one type of social organization (*Gemeinschaft*) to another (*Gesellschaft*) (Tonnies, 1887/1957).

Scollon and Scollon (1995) use this dichotomy to talk about discourse systems and how people learn to be members of these systems. Everyone is born into and grows up within a natural community and learns its rules *(Gemeinschaft)*. You can also join a goal-oriented community, such as an academic discourse community or a corporation *(Gesellschaft)*. The two systems are quite different and the ways in which people are socialized into them are different. *Gemeinschaft* and *Gesellschaft* are also useful, the Scollons point out, for distinguishing between goal-oriented professional communities. Asian businesses are more likely to be organized according to *Gemeinschaft* and Western businesses according to *Gesellschaft*. There are potential problems lurking for staff that move between the two systems.

One very useful and influential model of cultures is that of Edward Hall (1976), who talks about **high-context** and **low-context messages**. In a high-context message, there is little information in the message but lots in the context or in the persons. Hall gives the example of the law in the United States and France. Americans are proud of the fact that their government is impersonal; in the old saying it is "a government of laws, not men" (and women, as well). When someone is accused of a crime, the circumstances are deemed unimportant; whether the law was broken or not is, however, important. This is an example of low context. In France, on the other hand, gossip and hearsay are admitted, according to Hall, because the judge (who has greater powers than an American judge) wants to put the crime into (high) context. High-context messages often come out of relatively homogenous cultures such as Japan. In low-context messages, the information is in the language. Things must be made more explicit, such as in a computer program. Countries said to favor low-context messages are Germany and the United States.

Other fundamental oppositions or scales have been suggested in research on intercultural management. Categories from this sort of research may be useful for analyzing cultural differences. Hampden-Turner and Trompenaars (2000) have used the following six constructs in their research. It's important to note that these constructs do not exist separately but instead combine with each other to describe the attributes and styles of different cultures. It's also important to note that these are not value judgments but descriptions. There are good and bad aspects of each style.

- **Universalism—Particularism:** Universalist cultures stress the rules; for example, in these cultures even the head of government must answer to the law. Everyone gets treated the same way. Particularist cultures stress the fact that people are different and have to be treated in particular ways; connections matter and heads of state may break laws with impunity.

- **Individualism—Communitarianism:** Individualistic cultures see the individual as the most important unit of society. These cultures tolerate and even encourage dissent. Communitarian cultures think obligations to the society take precedence. Communitarian cultures subscribe to the adage, "It takes a village to raise a child."

- **Specificity—Diffuseness:** Cultures that admire **specificity** prefer an analytical approach. They tend to believe in progress and support research. Cultures that admire diffuseness prefer to look at the whole rather than the parts; they may favor a group decision-making process. This may be a good thing ("two heads are better than one") or a bad one ("paralysis by analysis," "two many cooks").

- **Achieved Status—Ascribed Status:** In cultures where achieved status is important, it matters most what you are or have become, while in cultures where ascribed status is important, your connections and lineage are important. The contrast here is between the ideology "anyone can grow up to be president" and the phenomenon of a dictator passing on the nation to his or her child.

- **Inner Direction—Outer Direction:** This distinction can be summarized in the contrast between the sayings "To thine own self be true" and "What will the neighbors think?" In some cultures, people are rewarded for following their consciences. In others, following one's own route is considered a selfish way to live. People think of their families and neighbors and rein in their behavior accordingly.

- **Sequential Time—Synchronous Time:** In cultures that follow the rules of sequential time, people prefer to do tasks one at a time. In **synchronous-time** cultures, a bank clerk may wait on several people and do several things at once and no one will complain.

As we have said, a given culture will combine these attributes, and we would add that members of that culture may not fit in with the dominant behavior.

Globalization and the Future of Cultures

Finally, we have to ask to what degree talk of cultures makes sense in a global world. Are we all becoming more alike? Is widespread travel and immigration having an effect on all of us? What about the Internet? Is there a *global village* emerging? The question is too large to tackle at this point, but we will note that a number of studies (Ess and Sudweeks 2001) have pointed out that computer-mediated communication (e.g., in chat rooms) is itself mediated by local conditions. That is, people chat as Thais, Indians, and Chinese. They may do so in English (though English is losing its initial predominance on the Internet) but may also keep and in fact use the Internet to help preserve their own cultures. Hongladarom (2001), for example, argues that Thai cultural attitudes mediate Western technology. In a case study of a newsgroup on Thailand and its culture, Hongladarom shows how the newsgroup was used to disseminate information about an event that was censored in the Thai press. The freedom of the net culture is encouraging some Thais to take a new look at the political process and their role in it. Thais are not just accepting "Western" notions of dissent blindly, however, but rather adapting them to circumstances. Hongladarom argues that the newsgroup also fosters a sense of community among its members, using the shifting of language between Thai and English (what we will later call *code switching*) as a resource to accomplish this. Just how much English should be used is itself a subject of much debate. Finally, Hongladarom sees the Internet as serving two functions, a globalizing one and a localizing one.

Teaching Scenarios

A teacher, who has been teaching for ten years, has always had a number of students from Latin America in her class. She now feels confident in making generalizations about how these students in particular learn. How valid is this? Think about the value of experience but also think about an individual student coming into the class for the first time. Is this situation similar to or different from the situation a younger sibling finds when taking a class from the same teacher as the older sibling?

 Check Your Knowledge

1. Articulate your understanding of both *stereotype* and *generalization*.
2. Summarize the findings of Nisbett, et al. (2001) with respect to Greek and Chinese civilizations, wholes and parts, explanations, and categorization.
3. Be able to define these terms:
   deficit model
   ethnocentrism
   high-context/low-context messages
   universalism/particularism
   individualism/communitarianism
   specificity/diffuseness
   achieved status/ascribed status
   inner direction/outer direction
   sequential time/synchronous time

Apply Your Knowledge

Look at the pairs of words below. Do you associate them with U.S. culture or with another culture or cultures? Do you associate the words with particular cultures? Work with a partner. Put the words into one of the two columns below.

individualism/community
fate/freedom
tradition/innovation
ascribed status/achieved status
inner directed/outer directed
cooperation/competition
idealistic/practical
religious/secular
hierarchy/equality
sequential time/synchronous time

U.S. culture	Another culture or cultures

Reflect

1. Do you think you are a good representative of your culture? Why or why not?
2. Consider the quotation from the beginning of the chapter by anthropologist Anthony Wallace who said that what is important is not the uniformity of the behavior of members of a given culture but rather the members' "capacity for mutual prediction." What does this mean? What are its implications?

Expand Your Knowledge

1. Investigate the claims made by Nisbett and his colleagues (2001, 2003). Use the references to read more on the subject, and then give a talk in class or write a paper about your findings.
2. How many cultures is your community home to? Investigate if there will be any cultural events or festivals held during this semester in your community.
3. Using the Internet, search for websites that address one of the issues raised in this chapter. In particular, you might want to find a site that compares American English and British English and determine if the generalizations made ring true for you. How would you modify what is presented in the site to make it more accurate?
4. If you have studied a foreign language, use the Internet to look up a country where that language is spoken. Does the site make any generalizations you find odd or at least untrue from your experience?
5. View a film, preferably one set in a different region or country from yours. What rules of language and culture do you observe in the film? Consider things such as greetings, how older people talk to younger people, how long the conversations are, etc. With a partner, think of as many rules of language and culture that you observed as you can. You may also

write a short paper about what you found. This book's northern author uses *To Kill a Mockingbird*. That film would not work in southern U.S. classrooms. Other possibilities are the *Star Wars* movies (or most science-fiction or fantasy movies).

Suggested Readings

Edward Hall. *Beyond Culture*. Garden City, NY: Doubleday, 1976.

Ronald Scollon and Suzanne Wong Scollon. *Intercultural Communication: A Discourse Approach*. 2d ed. Malden, MA: Blackwell, 2001.

Nature,
Language,
and Culture

2

1. What is language? What is culture?

2. How do people learn their first language and culture?

3. ⊞ Think of an adult you know (someone you know personally or a famous person; feel free to use yourself as an example) who speaks a second language. Did this person learn the second language as a child or an adult? How successful was the person in learning the second language? What factors do you think enabled the person to learn a second language?

Chapter 2 will help you understand the biological basis of language, including the theory of Universal Grammar and research on language learning with apes. The chapter also introduces the distinction between language and dialect and presents two contrasting views of culture. The relationship between language and culture is explored in a section on the Sapir-Whorf Hypothesis. Finally, we speculate about the role of identity in language and culture.

Nature and Language

Linguists consider language to be innate. Barring physical problems, all children learn to walk; barring extraordinary circumstances, all children learn to speak a first language. Intuitively, most people would say that children learn by imitating their parents. However, Noam Chomsky and others have raised "the logical problem" of language acquisition: children learn a complete language in about five years. This is more than could reasonably be expected given the input they receive.

Think about it: children listen to false starts, incomplete sentences, and odd constructions. Their grammar is seldom corrected, though their use of social conventions in speech, like politeness, often is corrected.

Yet children emerge with a more-or-less perfectly formed language. And perhaps most amazing, they are able to form new sentences that they couldn't possibly have heard before. How is this accomplished?

Since imitation cannot explain this phenomenon, linguists claim that humans are therefore genetically programmed to acquire language. In other words, humans do not have the language per se in their brains, but they have the capacity to acquire it readily and with minimal input. At one time, Chomsky spoke of a Language Acquisition Device (or LAD) in the brain. Now the principles that are hard-wired in our brains are called "Universal Grammar" or "generative grammar" (Radford 1997).

Another piece of evidence the followers of Chomsky have used for the existence of a biological basis for language is the **Critical Period Hypothesis (CPH).** In its strongest form, the CPH says that children must acquire their first language before puberty if they are ever to acquire it at all. A weaker version claims that first language acquisition will be more difficult after puberty. The CPH is partly based on a number of feral children—raised in the wild, supposedly by wolves, bears, tigers, and even gazelles—who have found their way to civilization. They have been able to learn isolated words and simple structures, but their language development has never approximated children of their own age. While it would seem that there is something to the weak version of the CPH, the fact that these children have been raised in harrowing circumstances leads one to believe that age is likely not the only factor at work. There are more than 50 documented examples of feral children. One of the most celebrated cases is from around 1800: Victor, "the Wild Boy of Aveyron," whose life was the subject of a classic film, *The Wild Child,* by the great French filmmaker Francois Truffaut. Victor was found on the outskirts of a small town and brought to Paris to Dr. Jean-Marc Itard, a pioneer in deaf education. Victor learned to recognize some written words but never acquired language. Between 1843 and 1895, 14 feral children were found in India; the best documented case was that of Amala and Kamala who were found by missionaries in India in 1920 (Fawcett, Ayrton, and White 1972; Candland 1993).

In the 1970s, linguists documented a modern case of a child raised in the most abusive of environments. "Genie" had learned no language at home and had been tied to a potty-chair or otherwise confined for almost 12 years. She was ultimately unable to make very little progress in learning language, though perhaps the custody battles that swirled around her caused the progress she was making to be less than what might have been possible ultimately (Curtiss 1977). Since the 1970s, there have been no widely documented examples of feral children.

In the earliest versions of Chomsky's work, he distinguished between *competence* and *performance*. **Competence** is the knowledge in our heads, what Chomsky later called "internal language." It is the ability to form correct sentences in our native languages. It is the ability to hear a sentence like *Running is the man* and intuitively know it's not a proper English sentence without having to analyze the positions of the subject and verb. **Performance** (external language) is actually saying sentences, using the language. Performance is variable while competence is not; if you're tired, you may well mispronounce a word but that has nothing to do with your competence in the language. It is also important here to note that our biological ability to acquire language is part of our human inheritance, not our individual heredity; if a child born of French parents were adopted by Chinese parents and raised in China, that child would speak Chinese.

Chomsky does not have much use for the field of sociolinguistics, which is, after all, the study of performance. Sociolinguists in turn have criticized Chomsky's notion of competence as narrow: Dell Hymes (1974) argued for the usefulness of the concept "communicative competence," which he defined as what a speaker had to know to be a member of a speech community. We will take up Hymes's ideas in some detail later (see Chapter 4).

If human beings are biologically predisposed to learn language, do they alone have language? What of the widely disseminated stories of apes who have been taught sign language or to otherwise communicate with humans? Some scientists have worked with dolphins. While we won't deny that communication between species has occurred, we hesitate to call what has passed between animals and their trainers as *language*. Different writers have counted various features of language that are unique to humans. We'll focus on those features that are characteristic of human language but are missing in ape communication.

The first two features of language unique to humans are linked in that both are concerned with the human ability to combine pieces of language, and to do so in innovative ways. The concept of *duality* says that language makes infinite use of finite sources. Language is built up from phonemes to morphemes and from morphemes to syntax or, in other words, from sounds to words to sentences. The concept of *productivity* says that it is always possible for speakers to produce a completely new sentence, one never heard before in that language. To prove that animals had language, you would have to show that they were capable of recombining signs in novel ways on a consistent basis.

Another important feature of human language is *displacement*. Language is used to talk about the past or future and about things that are not in front of us. Language can even be used to talk about the impossible. This is the feature of language that makes it possible to talk about language *as* language—*meta-language*. Finally, and importantly, language is culturally transmitted.

Perhaps the most successful attempt of an ape learning something like language was made by Kanzi, a bonobo. Sue Savage-Rumbaugh claims Kanzi learned to communicate in much the same way that children do, by observing and interacting with his mother. She also claims Kanzi was able to interpret English sentences that he heard for the first time. His abilities were discovered almost accidentally when his mother, who was being taught to communicate through lexigrams (symbols on a board), was briefly taken away to be bred (Savage-Rumbaugh, Shanker, and Taylor 1998).

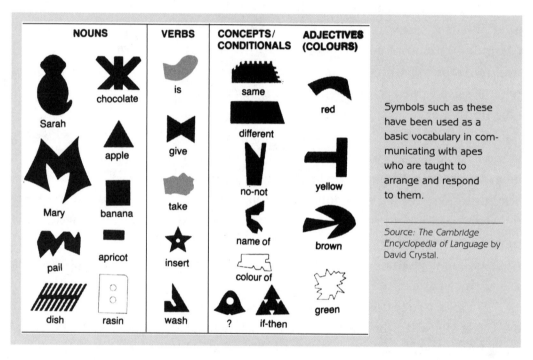

Symbols such as these have been used as a basic vocabulary in communicating with apes who are taught to arrange and respond to them.

Source: The Cambridge Encyclopedia of Language by David Crystal.

Lexigrams are distinctive shapes that represent words (a diamond for *go*, for example). They may be magnets or pictures laminated on a board. They are used to teach apes because ape vocal tracts are different from those of humans. Because of the placement of the base of the ape's tongue and its inability to completely close off the nasal cavity from the oral cavity, apes are physically incapable of making the sorts of sounds that are easy to discriminate. Some researchers have taught apes to use sign language, but apes' hands are not as good for signing as human hands are.

Kanzi pointed to symbols and sometimes combined them with gestures. He made phrases such as *melon go*, indicating that he wanted to go outside and eat watermelon. From the time he was 2½ years old to the time he was 9, Kanzi learned hundreds of lexigrams. At the age of 9, he was tested to see if he comprehended novel sentences, sentences he had never heard before such as *Put the toothbrush in the lemonade* and *Go scare Matata with the snake*. He was able to comprehend 72 percent of the sentences, a level of comprehension equal to that of a 2½-year-old child.

As impressive as his accomplishments are, Kanzi did not go as far in producing language as a normal child could, nor did he go at the same rapid pace. Critics say that Kanzi basically used lexigram and gesture combinations to get things he wanted or to get people to do things; that is, his language was limited to requests. He also did not understand grammar in the sense that the sentences he understood were not plausibly interchangeable. For example, *Grab Jeannine* and *Give the trash to Jeannine* require no processing of syntax; they can be understood as self-contained actions (Wallman 1992).

Yet, Savage-Rumbaugh points to the clumsiness of the board that contained the symbols the apes used to communicate to say that it made more wide-ranging conversation difficult, so that requests would necessarily be greater in number. She also points out a very interesting behavior of Kanzi's: He would seem to "talk" to himself using the board, pointing to his favorite things, such as *ball*. In some sense, therefore, the symbols had meaning for him as names of things.

Language and Dialect

So far, we have been speaking of language in its universal sense. But a variety of languages exist; a good guess is that there are about 6,000 languages still living, though large numbers of them are dying out, as we will later see (see Chapter 7). Appendix A lists the language families of the world.

Defining *language* can be slippery. **Language** can be contrasted with **dialect**. Languages are generally defined socially and politically. Thus, what makes Dutch and German separate languages, even though speakers of both can understand each other, is a long history, in each case, of autonomy and separateness. Every country has a number of dialects, based on accent, word choice, and grammar. In the United States, for example, we can get a good idea of where a person comes from by what he or she calls a carbonated beverage (e.g., *pop, soda, cold drink, dope*).

With the rise of mass media, however, some of these regional dialects are disappearing but a number of social dialects remain (see Chapter 7).

Related to the concept of language and dialect are the terms standard and nonstandard language. A **standard language** is the dialect with the most prestige in a community. A **nonstandard language** is a variety that is stigmatized or otherwise regarded as inferior. Note that evaluations by the community make languages standard or nonstandard; the terms have no basis otherwise.

The Nature of Culture

Culture has been defined using a number of metaphors: a road map, a recipe, a grammar. *Big-C Culture* has been used to describe the best artistic products of a society; to many, opera and ballet are Culture while country music is not. (We— and others—beg to differ.) *Small-c culture* is often what students of foreign languages are told they are studying when teachers bring in pictures of people in folk costumes. Historically, the concept of culture has been used to explain away differences between people; during colonialism, *culture* was what the colonized had. Culture has also been used to explain away problems in society; *the culture of welfare* and *the culture of crime* have been used to label, and thus explain (and not deal with), difficult social issues for years in the United States.

But, culture is much more than any of these things. Consider two definitions of culture:

> . . . that complex whole which includes knowledge, belief, art, law, morals, custom and any other capabilities and habits acquired by man as a member of society.
>
> (Tylor 1871)

> Culture is best seen not as complexes of concrete behavior patterns—customs, usages, traditions, habit clusters, as has been the case up to now, but as a set of control mechanisms— plans, recipes, rules, instructions (what computer engineers call 'program')—for governing behavior.
>
> (Geertz 1973)

It would be wrong to read the differences between the two definitions as progress—as in, we used to think one way and now we know better. Rather, they represent two ways of thinking about culture, both still intellectually active.

Culture Transmitted

The tradition of anthropology identified with the early 20th century anthropologist Franz Boas in the United States took culture to be a kind of knowledge that was learned and transmitted from one generation to another. Culture was seen as arbitrary; a child raised in a given culture would acquire it regardless of genetics. Children of expatriate parents usually acquire the culture they play in; if their playmates belong to the host culture that is what they will acquire. If the children play with children of other expatriates and are isolated from the host culture, they will acquire either their parents' culture or some hybrid international-community culture.

In this tradition, culture is "unnatural," and that's largely a good thing. Some philosophers claim that by being a member of a culture, people begin to take perspective; they get out of their own skins and appreciate what others are thinking and feeling.

Culture is a tool for classification and, as such, is an organizing tool. It helps organize our world, often through language. This approach to culture led anthropologists to search for different codings of kinship terms, for example. Who is called *mother* in a culture? Who is an *aunt*? Kinship terms are not, of course, the only words that operate this way. The verb *to drink* in Japanese (*nomu*) is used to talk both about drinking and taking medicine, while in English we would never say *I drank an aspirin*.

A second perspective on culture as transmitted knowledge is from cognitive anthropology. An early cognitive anthropologist, Goodenough, said that "a society's culture consists of whatever it is one has to know or believe in order to operate in a manner acceptable to its members" (1964, 36). People have to know two types of knowledge, then, propositional knowledge and procedural knowledge. Propositional knowledge is *knowledge that*. An example of such knowledge is *Dogs are pets*. By having this knowledge, people in a certain culture behave in a certain way, a way quite different from the people in a culture that has the knowledge *Dogs are food*. Procedural knowledge is *knowledge how*. Knowing how to go shopping in an open-air market versus how to behave in a supermarket are examples of procedural knowledge.

In its later form, cognitive anthropology became much more interested in schema or scripts. A schema is an abstract mental representation that we build up as a result of our experiences. For example, every American has a script *for ordering in a fast food restaurant*. You know what to expect when you walk in the door—what the clerks will say and in what order, more or less. If you are brave and go into a fast food restaurant in a country where you don't speak the language, you may well be able to get a meal just through your script knowledge, insofar as the routines are exported along with the burger franchises.

Culture Negotiated

Another tradition says culture is at some level negotiated. Geertz (1973) talks about the webs of meaning that exist between and among members of a culture. Culture, in this view, comes about as a result of human interaction. Perhaps what makes this view especially interesting is its insistence that after culture is created, it must be interpreted by its members. In this way, it goes beyond the idea that culture is knowledge. We must know how to behave as a member of a culture, but we also must know what it means when we act that way.

Others would agree, but they phrase things a bit differently. Researchers working with the ideas of the Russian psychologist Lev Vygotsky say that knowledge is social. Vygotsky is perhaps best known for the idea of the Zone of Proximal Development (ZPD), which has had a great influence in education. The ZPD is "the distance between the actual developmental level as determined by independent problem solving and the level of potential development as determined through problem solving under adult guidance [for children] or in collaboration with more capable peers" (Vygotsky 1978, 86). Thus, there is a difference between what one can do on one's own and with someone else (e.g., "Two heads are better than one"). The metaphor most commonly used to describe this process of helping learners through the ZPD is "scaffolding." The learner is supported by the adult or peer through questioning, coaching, and other appropriate means. Vygotsky felt that the child's internal or "intrapsychological" development was preceded by social or "interpsychological" development. That is, social learning is prior to and facilitates individual learning. Knowledge is itself facilitated by the psychological tools (like language and literacy) that people use, in the situations (like small groups) that they share, in the joint activity (like engaging in narratives) they engage in when headed for a common goal, and in the institutions of society. Cultural knowledge is in the interaction between and among all these factors (Tomasello 1999).

In addition to the metaphors of scaffolding and psychological tools, and instead of metaphors such as computer programs or guidebooks, researchers in this tradition use the metaphor of apprenticeship. People learn culture through interacting with each other; the process is at least as important as the product. We can see apprenticeship at work when children help parents cook, or when parents play cars with their children, implicitly teaching stories and appropriate interactional styles (Lave and Wenger 1991; Rogoff 2003).

Thus, Ochs (1988) points out that socialization, taken to be the teaching of culture to the young, is really "a lifespan experience." Through interaction, members of a given culture socialize and are socialized by others. Culture emerges through action while it is simultaneously organizing action, offering its members a perspective on the meaning of that action.

Accounts of culture in this negotiated tradition remind us that cultures, because they are tied to action/participation, have histories. They are not abstract, status-quo products. Such accounts remind us that humans have agency; we are not passive hostages of culture but rather active makers of it.

The Relationship between Language and Culture

The recent expansion of the European Union has led to a greater role for English within the organization and a subsequent diminution of the role of French, as many of the diplomats from the new member states are more likely to be fluent in English than in French. This has raised the issue of the connection between language and culture. French officials have worried that it might be impossible to speak English without "thinking American." What these officials are claiming is a version of the **Sapir-Whorf Hypothesis**. The hypothesis had two parts. The first part was the idea of *linguistic relativity;* languages had categories, grammatical structures, and other distinctions that were not found in other languages. Because different groups have different languages, they see the world differently. As Edward Sapir said, "No two languages are ever sufficiently similar to be considered as representing the same social reality. The worlds in which different societies live are distinct worlds, not merely the same world with different labels attached" (Mandelbaum 1949).

The second part of the Sapir-Whorf Hypothesis was the idea of *linguistic determinism,* the notion that language determines thought; we think in a certain way and can only think in that way because of the language we speak. In the strongest version of the hypothesis, translation was impossible. For example, the fact that Coeur d'Alene (western U.S.) requires (according to Whorf) distinctions between three causal processes denoted by three causal verbs does not square with the English word *cause.* The strong version of the Sapir-Whorf Hypothesis is no longer widely accepted, but the weak version, the idea that language influences (but does not determine) thought, has become part of the general intellectual makeup of our times.

Sapir was a student of Franz Boas, and it was a small illustration in one of Boas's books that came to epitomize the Sapir-Whorf Hypothesis. Boas was discussing the ways language can encode ideas through morphology. He pointed out that the idea of water takes many separate forms in English such as WATER, RIVER, LAKE, RAIN, and DEW. He went on to say that "it is perfectly conceivable that this variety of ideas, each of which is expressed by a single independent term in English, might be expressed in other languages by derivation from the same term" (Boas 1911/1966).

For example, Boas said, Eskimos (the people now called Inuit, who live in Canada) treat words for snow in this way.

> *Aput* is SNOW ON THE GROUND.
> *Qana* is FALLING SNOW.
> *Piqsirpoq* is DRIFTING SNOW.
> *Qimuqsuq* is SNOW DRIFT.

The meaning rested in a root that was inflected in different ways to convey different meanings. This would be as if *river* in English were WATERING or *lake* were WATER STANDING STILL. This simple point about morphology was expanded in the mind of the public to "Eskimos have 50 (or 5,000) words for snow." It turns out there are just two *roots* for snow in a standard dictionary of Eskimo: *qanik* (SNOW IN THE AIR) and *aput* (SNOW ON THE GROUND) (Martin 1986; Pullum 1991).

Sapir and Benjamin Lee Whorf went beyond Boas to claim that experience was mediated through language. This is what came to be known as the strong version of the Sapir-Whorf Hypothesis. We think only in ways that our language allows us. Whorf claimed that dividing snow into SNOW ON THE GROUND, FALLING SNOW, and so on showed the Inuit had a unique vision of the world that another culture would not necessarily be able to understand. Others since his time have pointed out that average English speakers know a lot of words for snow (e.g., *sleet, slush, blizzard*), and skiers know even more.

In "The Relation of Habitual Thought and Behavior to Language," Whorf contrasted what he called *Standard Average European* (SAE), a generalization built up from analysis of European languages, with Hopi, an Indian language of the southwestern United States, to show how certain linguistic meanings lead to certain kinds of thought. (See Carroll 1956.)

SAE, for example, allows plurals for both real objects and imaginary ones. That is, in English, for example, you can count ten men or ten days. In Hopi, plurals (and cardinal numbers *one, two, three*) are used only for real things. To count days, Hopis, claimed Whorf, would have to say something like *the tenth day*. For Whorf, this showed that the Hopi experience time subjectively, as a "becoming."

Whorf also claimed that Hopi terms for phases of time such as *summer* or *morning* are not nouns, as they are in SAE, but a kind of adverb *(when it is hot/when it is early in the day)*.

Whorf next contrasted tenses and aspects in SAE and Hopi, arguing that while SAE has three tenses (past, present, future), Hopi has two, the past/present and the future, roughly corresponding to what is or has been experienced and what is expected.

These examples led Whorf to contrast the habitual thoughts of the speakers of SAE and Hopi. SAE is lived in a world of objects while Hopi is lived in a world of events. The two world views seemed to him irreconcilable. In "An American Indian Model of the Universe," Whorf implied that a physicist speaking SAE could not communicate with a physicist speaking Hopi because their assumptions would be so different.

Language, Culture, and Identity

Whorf's work fell out of favor for a number of years but has been recently extended in interesting ways (Lucy 1992; Gumperz and Levinson 1996; Gentner and Goldin-Meadow 2003). Language and culture is again a "hot" topic. Nevertheless, some have begun to question at least one fundamental assumption of the Sapir-Whorf Hypothesis: the isomorphic match between one culture and one language. There is no necessary connection. People are often bilingual and bicultural. On the other hand, people may be ignorant of a language and still participate in the culture of that language. A third-generation immigrant may know very little of the language of ancestors and still participate fully in cultural rituals and celebrations.

It would obviously be wrong to say that language and culture, singularly or combined, account for everything in human behavior. Ethnicity, religion, gender, and socioeconomic status (class) are all large parts of our identities as people. All may be implicated in success at school. Teachers may find that groups presumed to be unified or monolithic are deeply divided. As Americans well know, there are sometimes racial boundaries within a culture that are hard to cross. Racial divisions exist in many countries; in South America, advancement to higher education may be facilitated by membership in the white community and impeded by membership in the Native American community. In the realm of religion, there are differences between Sunni and Shiite Muslims, between Roman Catholic and Protestant Christians, and between Orthodox and Reform Jews. Attitudes toward gender may cause differential treatment between individuals and in classrooms. The individual's willingness to follow the behavior associated with gender in a given society may have an impact on his or her life. Class is another factor in identity. Teachers of international students may think of all members of one culture as undifferentiated, but there may be large class differences within the culture that have constrained an individual's life experience (differences that may interact with those of race, religion, and gender).

In the case of people learning another language, issues of identity are intertwined with motivations for learning the language. The goals of students who are learning English before attending American universities from which they will graduate and return home are different from the goals of refugee and immigrant students. Researchers in second language learning find it axiomatic that students of second languages and foreign languages require separate methods and materials. *Second languages* are those spoken as important languages in the country where they are being learned; teaching English to immigrants from Africa in the United States is English as a second language. *Foreign languages* are languages not widely spoken in the country of instruction; high school students studying French in the United States learn French as a foreign language, as do Japanese college students studying French in Tokyo.

The theme of construction of identity runs, implicitly and explicitly, throughout this textbook. Identity involves language, culture, and the variables we have discussed here—and many more.

Cultural Universals

Finally, to complete this discussion, we need to mention that a number of cultural universals have been postulated—among them the existence of personal names, beliefs about death, classification schemes of plants and animals, a division of labor, narrative—and cultural variability as a universal itself! We will address universals and particulars in some depth in Chapters 3 and 9.

Teaching Scenarios

1. Remember the scenario from Chapter 1, in which a teacher made predictions about new Latin American students based on her experience with similar students over time. What additional information in this chapter can you bring to your answer? How would you answer the question from Chapter 1 now?

2. A teacher says this to you: "I work hard at developing a good classroom culture." In the context of this chapter, what might that teacher mean in terms of (a) transmitted culture and (b) negotiated culture? How does the concept of socialization apply?

☑ Check Your Knowledge

1. What evidence exists for the biological basis of language?
2. Why do we say that apes can communicate but do not have language?
3. What is the difference in perspective between viewing culture as transmitted knowledge and culture as negotiated?
4. What is the Sapir-Whorf Hypothesis?
5. Are language and culture the only factors that explain human behavior?
6. Be able to define these terms:
   Critical Period Hypothesis
   competence/performance (internal language/external language)
   language
   dialect
   schema

Apply Your Knowledge

What do you need to study culture? What kind of evidence would be most useful? Think of U.S. culture or any other culture you know well. Make a list of things that are symbolic of that culture. One way to think about this is to plan a time capsule that will be buried and dug up in 200 years. What would you include so that people could reconstruct what the culture was like? Try to use actual credible publications. Don't simply list several reference books or websites.

Reflect

What do you think (or know) that people find strange about American culture? Is there something about another culture you have never been able to understand?

Expand Your Knowledge

1. Find the children's book *Fish Is Fish* by Leo Lionni in the library. Work with a partner to discuss the story, or write a short essay about the connection between the story and the ideas in this chapter.

2. There have been many accounts of language learning by apes. Investigate one case and report to the class or write a paper about it.

3. 🖥 Using the Internet, find at least two sites that concern themselves with language or culture. What sort of information is found on each site?

4. Frances FitzGerald began her 1972 book *Fire in the Lake* with a chapter called "States of Mind." In it, she argued that the Vietnam War was fought in the midst of a vast misunderstanding rooted in cultural differences. Though many Americans learned to speak Vietnamese, "the language gave no more than a hint of the basic intellectual grammar that lay beneath" (FitzGerald 1972, 7). Vietnam was an agricultural society whose notions of time and space were fundamentally different from those of the United States. FitzGerald's chapter is an interesting meditation on the extremes to which intercultural misunderstandings can lead. Read FitzGerald's chapter and apply the ideas of this chapter to it. (You may also want to look at Thomas L. Friedman's *Longitudes and Attitudes* for another, more recent, example.)

Suggested Readings

David Crystal. *The Cambridge Encyclopedia of Language.* 2d ed. Cambridge: Cambridge University Press, 1997.

Clifford Geertz. "Deep Play: Notes on the Balinese Cockfight." In *The Interpretation of Cultures.* New York: Basic Books, 1973.

Ellen McIntyre, Ann Rosebery, and Norma Gonzalez. *Classroom Diversity: Connecting Curriculum to Students' Lives.* Portsmouth, NH: Heinemann, 2001.

Steven Pinker. *The Language Instinct.* New York: William Morrow, 1994.

Words across Cultures

1. When you hear these words, what do you "see"?

   bird, dog, tree

2. Think about the last time you gave directions. What elements did you include in your direction giving?

3. ⊞ Work in groups of three. Think of as many proverbs as you can. Once you've finished brainstorming, group the proverbs. Which seem to go together? Now think of a label to apply to each grouping. What cultural value is expressed in each group? What do proverbs say about U.S. culture?

Chapter 3 will help you understand the different meanings and associations that words can have in a given language. It will also help you understand how words can be compared across languages. The chapter accomplishes these goals by exploring cultural universals and particulars as they are manifested in common word sets such as colors, family terms, and spatial vocabulary. Finally, we look at issues in translation.

Word Meanings

What do the following words have in common?

> *slime*
> *sludge*
> *slug*
> *slither*
> *sloppy*

You probably first answered, "They all begin with *sl*—." True enough, but what sense or feeling do they share? If you take a moment more to think about that, you'll probably answer that they are all rather unpleasant words. An author trying to convey a bad initial impression of a character or place might well use a word beginning with *sl*—. J. K. Rowling, the author of the *Harry Potter* books, named the evil dormitory *Slytherin*, for example. Other examples are the vowel sounds in *teeny, weeny,* and *wee* and in *grand* and *vast*. If someone were to make up a new English word, *neek*, our first impression of it might well be that it named something small.

But what of the words *slim* or *knee*? Do they follow the rules above? Clearly not. While languages sometimes have a preference for linking certain sounds and meanings, ultimately, linguistic signs are arbitrary. This is one of the cardinal insights in linguistics; it was enunciated by Ferdinand de Saussure (1915/1959). An English speaker sees a dog walking down the street, sleeping on the floor, or digging in the garden and calls it a *dog*. A French speaker calls the same animal *chien*, a Japanese speaker *inu*, and a Spanish speaker *perro*. There is nothing inherent in a dog that makes one label correct. The label assigned dogs by different languages is an arbitrary one. This is true even in the case of onomatopoeia, or sound symbolism. English speakers think we are reproducing the sound of a dog barking when we say *bow wow*. Japanese speakers think they have it right when they use the words *wan wan*, as do the French when they use *ouah ouah*.

Even among speakers of the same language, however, *dog* has different meanings. We certainly all agree on the dictionary definition of *dog* (a member of the species *Canis familiaris*). This dictionary definition is known to linguists as the word's **denotation.**

All words have meanings beyond their denotations; these are the **connotations** of the word. If you were bitten by a dog as a child, you may have an individual connotation for *dog* that is less pleasant than the one held by someone whose experience with dogs is attack free. Connotations of words may change over time. Calling a person *dog* has been an insult (*You dirty dog*), a term of address (*Yo dog!*), and a term of endearment (*He's my dog; you lucky dog*) in American English over the years.

Connotations have cultural aspects as well as personal and temporal aspects. The color white is associated with purity in Western cultures but is associated with death in many Asian cultures. Red is the color of celebration and luck in China, but it is the color of danger/warning, Christmas, and Valentine's Day in the United States.

Ways of Comparing Words

We need ways to consider word meanings in order to make words comparable across cultures. This sort of research was frequently done in the 1960s and 1970s under the name *ethnosemantics*. One important idea was classification systems. A taxonomic classification system arranges things in hierarchies. For example, anthropologists are often interested in how people name plants. In English, we have categories such as *tree, bush, shrub,* and *plant*. In the *tree* category, we have pines, oaks, elms, and so on, and each of these categories can be further divided. Within a given culture, people who garden or hike will have more names for plants than people who do not go outdoors very often, but cultures themselves will clearly differ on how they divide up the natural world. Taxonomic systems help us understand how the division is done. Within taxonomies, we can also see how synonyms are distinguished by their connotations. For example, plants may have scientific names and colloquial names, and people might use different terms at different times *(rhododendrum/rhodie)*. In another sort of classification system, the constituent classification system, we can clearly view how languages label parts. For example, in English, the knuckle is a part of the finger, which is part of the hand. A language may have just a single word for the entire area from fingertip to shoulder, or one word for what English separates into hip and buttocks.

Another way words are distinguished is through **semantic feature analysis.** To return to our *dog* example (sorry, cat lovers), a dog is defined as

> [+ canine], [+ domesticated]
> to distinguish it from the wolf, which is
> [+ canine], [– domesticated].

Though this approach was once widely used, it is now criticized as inefficient. There are just too many pluses and minuses necessary to differentiate most closely related words.

Another way to look at meaning is through the concept of a prototype. Prototype theory says that not all members of a category are equal, in the sense that there are better and worse examples of a category. **Prototypes** are the "best" examples of a category. For example, the classic experiments of Rosch (1973) found that in the United States apples were prototypical fruits, robins prototypical birds, and carrots prototypical vegetables. That is, when people were asked for examples of a category, these examples were named first and fastest. In this view of meaning, membership in a category is not a matter of checking off a list of features but rather a matter of reference points, with membership being a matter of similarity to the reference points, the prototypes (Lobner 2002).

Universals and Particulars, Revisited: Color Terms

Because linguistic signs are arbitrary and because connotations are cultural, we would expect the meanings of words to change across given cultures. Yet, human beings clearly share an enormous amount, including the same biology and the same needs. Is it really possible that words centered on our most basic humanity are perceived differently by different cultures? This question has been investigated using color terms, kinship terms, spatial orientation, and emotions.

All human eyes, of course, are capable of perceiving the same colors. That is part of our shared biology. (Clearly, some people are color-blind, but that's a different story.) However, Berlin and Kay (1969) showed that different cultures see different colors in the sense that they classify them differently, albeit within a relatively narrow range of possibilities. (So in that sense color is a universal.) They also said that there is an implicational scale of color terms; that we can predict the occurrence of a color set within a given culture. Physiologically, the human eye sees six basic colors: red, yellow, green, blue, white, and black. Obviously, colors get combined, and we are able to see those colors too. Colors are described in terms of their hue (quality or –*ness*), their brightness (ability to reflect light), and their saturation (strength—vivid to pastel).

Berlin and Kay and others have used a set of 330 color chips, varying in hue and brightness, all at maximum saturation, to test how different languages (more than 100 at last count) name colors. They found that languages varied, with some having two basic color terms and others having up to 11 such terms.

Basic color terms were defined as:

- one morpheme (no *blue-green* or *bluish*);
- not a hyponym (subset) of another color (no *scarlet*, which is a kind of red, or *lime*, which is a kind of green);
- unrestricted in use (no *blonde* because it is only used to describe hair color/complexion and is not a color you'd paint your house);
- "psychologically salient" (remembered often or named as among the first of a set of terms; no *teal*).

Though they claimed that these four criteria were enough to decide most cases, they also said that basic color terms could not include a metaphor (no *plum*, named after the fruit, or *gold*, where the name of the substance is identical to the color name) or a term recently borrowed from another language (in English, no *beige*, which is borrowed from the French).

It seems that languages tend to agree on focal colors, the best examples of hues. When asked by experimentees to find "the best" red, for example, members of different cultures agreed that fire-engine red is a good red. This was true no matter how many basic colors the culture had (assuming it indeed had red). Berlin and Kay said there was also a pattern across colors, an implicational scale that says if a culture has one color, it will have another, as shown in the following scale.

- *Two color words:* Dani (Papua New Guinea). Dani uses the word *mili* for black, dark browns, and cool colors (like blue) and the word *mola* for white, light browns, and warm colors (like red).
- *Three color words:* Swahili (Africa) and Pomo (California) have words for white, black, and red.
- *Four color words:* The next stage has yellow or GRUE (a green-blue category in which both colors have the same name, as in old Japanese, where *aoi* sufficed for both the color of trees and the sea) but not both. Hanunoo (Philippines) has white, black, red, and GRUE. Bisayan (Philippines) has white, black, red, and yellow.
- *Five color words:* Paez (Colombia) and Ixcatec (Mexico) have black, white, red, GRUE, and yellow, which is the most common pattern for the following step.

- *Six color words:* Green and blue are differentiated next. This is the system of Mandarin (China) and Masai (Sudan).
- *Seven color words:* Brown is added in the next stage, which is used by Javanese (Indonesia) and Bari (Sudan).
- *Eleven color words:* Finally, purple, pink, orange, and gray are added, usually together. (English, Spanish, Korean).

Though Berlin and Kay's findings are accepted by most linguists and anthropologists, they have had their critics (Kay and Maffi 2000). For example, critics have asked what it means for a culture to have a given color. Colors are much more than hues, as we have seen with the widely varying connotations for *white*. Furthermore, colors need to be understood in relation to other colors; white is white, but it is also not black or red. Others have questioned the very concept of a basic color, saying it makes little sense from a cultural point of view to differentiate basic colors from secondary colors.

Universals and Particulars, Revisited: Family Terms

Color is one universal of human experience. Family life of some sort is seen as another. Motherhood is probably universal; people around the world would identify the birth mother as *mother*, at least up to some point where adoption or a blending of families takes place. Fatherhood is not nearly so universal. For example, in the traditional culture of the Nayar (India), which has now disappeared, a prepubescent girl was ritually united with a young man, who left after the four-day ceremony. The young woman was then free to enter into other relationships. The children of any of the woman's relationships owed certain ritual obligations to that young man with whom the mother was ceremonially linked; in certain areas, the children called him by the title *appan*.

The Na people of southern China have no acknowledged fathers and no husbands. Men visit women in the middle of the night. There are no nuclear families. Brothers, sisters, and close maternal relatives live together in a household.

Hungarians had no terms for brother and sister until the 19th century, using a word like *sibling*, though they did have terms for *older sibling* and *younger sibling*. The Swedes have separate words for each grandparent: *farfar, morfar, farmor,* and *mormor* (father's father, mother's father, father's mother, and mother's mother).

It seems clear that kinship is a social construct and that different cultures put people in different categories. That is, people are defined socially (by their roles) rather than geneologically (by their place on a chart). Why that is so has been extensively argued; do words for family reflect social obligations and relationships? Does the fact that in some societies you call your father and your father's brother by the same title imply a particular closeness or a particular obligation on the part of the father's brother? No solutions are offered here, but we do outline some kinship terminology systems to underscore the relativity and social nature of such terms.

Many cultures tend to separate lineal relatives (parents, grandparents) and collateral relatives (uncles, aunts, cousins). This is the system for English (anthropologists call it the Eskimo system of kinship). There are some minor differences across cultures within this system. We have seen the example of the Swedish language, which has separate names for each grandparent. The Swedish system of lineal/collateral works just the same as that of English, however. Japanese makes a distinction between older and younger brothers (*ani, otooto*) and older and younger sisters (*ane, imooto*), but the system is, again, basically the same as that of English.

There are other ways to organize family terminology. In Hawaiian culture, age is important, and all male relatives of one's parents' generation are called by the term *father*. All female relatives of one's parents' generation are called by the term *mother*. In what anthropologists call the Iroquois system, it is with the sides of the family, father's and mother's, that the distinctions lie; the same word is used for *father* and *father's brother*, with a different word being used for *mother's brother*. *Mother* and *mother's sister* share a word different from *father's sister.* Several Melanesian (southern Pacific) languages share this system. In the Crow system (central United States), terms cross generations, so that a woman would use the same term for her brother and her son. The details of the several systems need not concern us. The point we wish to make is that it is possible to view and label family relationships in various ways.

Clearly, parents do ask their children to call the parents' friends *Uncle Jay* and *Aunt Sally*. In North American culture, this appropriation of kinship titles for friends is usually done on a case-by-case basis. However, African Americans will often call each other *sister* or *brother* to create a feeling of solidarity. In Chinese culture, this use of titles is ritualized: shop clerks and people on the street may be addressed *big sister* or *uncle* with respect rather than intimacy implied. We will look at terms of address more fully in Chapter 4.

Universals and Particulars, Revisited: Space

Still another universal experience is orientation in space. Because humans all have the same bodies, we would expect universal agreement on terms such as left/right and front/back. This is not the case, however. Some languages, including some in Australia, South Asia, and Mesoamerica, have absolute viewpoints on spatial orientation, much like the north/south/east/west of English, that do not change based on where you are standing. For example, Guugu Yimithirr (northeastern Australia) uses a directional system based on a horizontal plane. So, something that is *to the north* is always to the north, whether it's currently behind you or in front of you, to your left or right (Levinson 1997). Speakers carry a mental map in their heads. In mountainous countries, uphill and downhill may be the prime orienting directions. Close objects are downhill, whereas far ones are uphill. It's important to emphasize that the speakers of these languages are not using landmarks, as we might when hiking, but are instead carrying a conceptual map in their heads. Levinson and his colleagues (2002) report a Tenejapan Tzeltal (Mexico) speaker in an unfamiliar city asking whether the hot tap was the uphill or downhill one. Clearly the speaker has no mountains in the hotel room to orient by but is instead using an internal map.

Research reported by Pederson and his colleagues (1998) tested speakers of Dutch and Japanese, who have relative terms such as left and right, and speakers of Tzeltal (Mexico) and Longgu (Pacific), who have absolute systems. The subjects were asked to observe a line of toy animals on a table. The subjects were then turned around 180 degrees to face another table and asked to put the toys in the same order as on the original table. Speakers of the relative languages tended to use their own bodies for orientation, so that a toy facing left originally would still face left. Speakers of absolute languages tended to put toys originally facing left facing to the right on the second table, so that their position did not change.

Universals and Particulars, Revisited: Mental States

Surely mental states are part of our human heritage, more nature than nurture. Work across cultures makes this too seem questionable. Schieffelin (1985) placed feelings in the sociocultural context of Kaluli (Papua New Guinea) life, showing that emotions are social as well as psychological; people get angry or feel shame for a purpose. Lutz (1988) showed how emotions are socially constructed, using as her example *rus* among the Ifaluk people of the Solomon Islands. *Rus* is a sort of panic attack that can incapacitate people or cause them to run around, making little sense. The 1994 edition of the mental health handbook, *The Diagnostic and Statistical Manual of Mental Disorders*, indeed recognized "culture-bound syndromes." These syndromes are controversial among mental health professionals, but they are interesting to contemplate for the claim that certain cultures have unique kinds of dysfuntional behaviors. *Anorexia nervosa* occurs frequently among young American women. *Amok* (which has been taken into English in the term *to run amok*) is a Malaysian condition characterized by a sudden uncontrollable anger; people with this condition have been known to kill whomever they see in a bout of rage. West African men suffer *brain fag* (fag = tired in British English), a condition whereby they cannot concentrate and have blurred vision. In Latin America, people have *susto*, a state of extreme fear in which they believe their souls have been stolen. These examples show that people in different cultures do not organize their experiences in the same ways.

We will next consider another supposed universal, the use of metaphors within given cultures. We do so admitting that work in this field has been limited mostly to western contexts.

Metaphor

What are the figurative meanings of these old proverbs?

> *Cleanliness is next to Godliness.*
> *A penny saved is a penny earned.*

What do they tell us about the culture that recites them? What cultural values are inherent in the sayings? Proverbs provide insight into culture. In a similar way, so do metaphors. **Metaphors** are figures of speech that equate one thing with another. *This test is a piece of cake* means it is easily handled, as pleasant as eating cake. *Bob is a bear without his coffee* means that Bob is surly without his caffeine.

In *Metaphors We Live By*, Lakoff and Johnson (1980) analyzed a number of metaphors central to North American culture. One of their central organizing principles is that metaphor is rooted in the human body, with *up* more exalted than *down*. **More is up, less is down:** *His diploma opened up a lot of opportunities. The teacher closed down the discussion when things got too heated.* **Good is up, bad is down:** *look up to, look down on*.

Another central insight of Lakoff and Johnson's work was the approach to communication implicit in our use of metaphors. Communication is seen as the passing on of ideas (seen as objects) in sentences (seen as containers) through conduits: *I get your meaning. I lost my chain of thought.* Several scholars have commented on how this conduit metaphor for communication slights the view of communication as a co-construction based on the hearer's understanding of the speaker's message. Adopting either metaphor of communication has consequences for the ways we use and teach about language in the classroom.

Perhaps the most cited and reproduced section of Lakoff and Johnson's book is the part discussing the central metaphor *Argument is war*. You win arguments by *shooting down* others. You *attack* indefensible claims. Comments are *right on target*. An understanding of such metaphors is part of the competence a learner of any foreign language must acquire. An understanding of this particular metaphor would clearly be of use to anyone trying to participate in American academic culture.

Translation

The consequences of the information found in this chapter for translating from one language and culture to another are perhaps obvious: any translation is a very difficult thing to accomplish. Some translations are clearly more difficult than others; if you are translating an instruction manual you will have fewer problems than if you are translating a poem. Culture matters little in the writing of an instruction manual, so the translator has mostly to worry about accuracy, not connotations or metaphors, in the translation (though there may be cases where the writer must be aware of these larger concerns). When cultural products are being translated, there are a number of issues to consider.

At a summit meeting in 1970, President Richard Nixon, who was under domestic political pressure from textile producers, asked Japanese Prime Minister Eisaku Sato to cut back Japan's textile exports. Sato responded with a phrase that was translated as *I'll do my best*. When later no action was taken by the Japanese government, Nixon was furious and felt betrayed. Commentators said that Sato had used a stock phrase that someone who knew Japanese culture would recognize as polite but meaningless in terms of any promise for action. Sato did not want to directly confront Nixon by saying he couldn't do anything, so he used a catch phrase instead, one apparently not fully understood by the American interpreters.

Becker (1995) points out that one of the prime difficulties in translation is "silence." One aspect of silence is what gets elaborated (or not) in individual languages; another aspect is the topics people can talk about and how. Becker gives an example of a reporter from the *New York Times* trying to interview a young dancer from Bali (Indonesia) through an interpreter. The reporter wanted to ask the dancer how long he had danced and how long he practiced each day. The reporter's questions were met by confusion on the part of the interpreter because there was no place for such questions in the context of the kind of training the young man had gone through. These were things that were not considered important to understanding the career of a dancer. The reporter was asking questions for a Western ballet dancer, not a Balinese dancer.

A related aspect of silence for Becker is that of intertextuality or prior text. He relates how as an ethnographer relatively skilled in speaking several Southeast Asian languages, he still cannot tell when people are quoting proverbs or pieces of ancient literature. He likens this to his saying "Seek and ye shall find" to someone who would think it was an original expression. The notion of prior text is related to the idea variously labeled *schema,* or *frames* (or, as we have seen, *scripts*). These terms refer to the fact that all of us have prior experiences that we encode as abstract representations in our minds. We have a *going out to the mall* script; we know there will be a large parking lot, a food court, some large department stores and general small ones, nearby chain restaurants, etc.

Sometimes the structure of the languages makes translating from one to the other difficult in quite fundamental ways. Slobin (1996) contrasted translations of novels from Spanish to English and English to Spanish. Both are, of course, Indo-European languages and thus related. Spanish verbs, however, behave differently from English ones. Romance languages like Spanish put core information in the verb, while English verbs put that information outside the verb, in a particle. Compare *entrar* (enter) and *subir* (ascend) with *go in* and *go up*. In the case of Spanish, the directional information is inside the verb, while in English it is within *in* and *up*, the particles.

In novels, sometimes the rest of the story makes the direction clear, so that the translator can omit it. Slobin (1996) considers the original sentence from John Fowles's *The French Lieutenant's Woman*: "Gradually he worked his way up to the front of the bluffs." This was translated into Spanish as "Poco a poco, fue acercándose hasta el pie de los riscos." Translating back into English, this is, "Gradually he was approaching the foot of the bluffs" (p. 210). Other times, information gets lost in translation. From the same novel, we have " . . . she moved out into the sun and across the stony clearing . . . " which was translated " . . . la muchacha salió al claro rocoso . . . " (the girl exited to the stony clearing) (p. 211). These are not bad translations; they are appropriate for their readers. A reader of Spanish would probably find the extra detail necessitated by a more literal translation to be confusing and an impediment to the flow of the story.

Teaching Scenarios

1. A tutor is working with a student on an essay. The tutor is explaining some mistakes in grammar that the student has made. The student repeatedly says "yes" after the tutor's explanations. The following week, many of the mistakes are left uncorrected or changed in ways that don't match the tutor's explanations. There are several possible reasons why this happened, but focus on the word "yes." What did the tutor think "yes" meant? What might the student have thought "yes" meant?

2. You invite a Chinese colleague to a meeting, and he is surprised that there are only two of you. He expected more people. Why might this have happened? What might "meeting" mean to him? What does it mean to you?

 ## Check Your Knowledge

1. What do we mean when we say that linguistic signs are arbitrary?

2. What is semantic feature analysis? Do a semantic feature analysis of the following pairs of words:
   cow/bull
   condominium/house

3. Briefly state the conclusion of Berlin and Kay's color studies.

4. Can we say it is true that the word *aunt* means the same thing to all people? Why or why not?

5. Can we say it is true that the words *right* and *left* mean the same things to all people? Why or why not?

6. Think of some examples from English that follow the metaphor **Good is up/bad is down**.

---

7. Be able to define these terms:

> *onomatopoeia*
>
> *denotation*
>
> *connotation*
>
> *prototype*
>
> *semantic feature analysis*
>
> *basic color term*
>
> *metaphor*

Apply Your Knowledge

1. Certain expressions shape culture. Brainstorm expressions in English that depend on violence (e.g., *in the trenches, on the front lines, pull your leg*). Now try to create peaceful equivalents for these expressions. Try using these newly created expressions outside of class and notice people's reactions. What do these expressions tell us about the conventions of language?
2. Think of the connotations for these colors: red, pink, green, lavender, yellow, white, black.

Reflect

Think of five key words that explain your culture. How would you explain these words to a visitor from another planet?

Expand Your Knowledge

1. Read Pederson et al. (1998), Li and Gleitman (2002), and Levinson et al. (2002) to get a sense of how people do research. Li and Gleitman criticize Perderson and his colleagues and offer new evidence, which is then critiqued by Levinson and his colleagues, who offer their own evidence. In a paper, summarize the argument and offer your own views based on the evidence.

2. Ask five men and five women to provide you with as many color names as they can. Are these what the chapter calls "basic colors"? What differences and similarities did you find in the way people responded?

3. ⌨ Do an online search for the use of kinship terms in different cultures. Report your findings.

4. ⌨ Go to a translation site. Type in a paragraph on the site and translate it into another language and then back into English. Compare the original and the back-translation. What do you conclude about the results (e.g., what sorts of things are difficult to translate)?

Suggested Readings

Anne Fadiman. *The Spirit Catches You and You Fall Down*: *A Hmong Child, Her American Doctors, and the Collision of Two Cultures*. New York: Farrar, Straus, and Giroux, 1997.

George Lakoff and Mark Johnson. *Women, Fire and Other Dangerous Things: What Categories Tell Us about the Mind.* Chicago: University of Chicago Press, 1987.

Sebastian Lobner. *Understanding Semantics*. New York: Oxford University Press, 2002.

Language and Interaction

1. What do you think it means when we say there are rules for conversation?

2. What are some things that irritate you about the way other people converse?

3. ⊞ Think of as many situations as you can when these phrases would be spoken:

    -   It's hot in here.
    -   What time is it?
    -   Did you do this?
    -   How long have you been driving?
    -   That's brilliant!

Chapter 4 will help you understand the idea of communicative competence. It explores how people cooperate when having conversations by using certain rules and devices. We also present important theories of speech acts, conversational implicature, and politeness.

Communicative Competence

In Chapter 2, we introduced the distinction Chomsky made between competence and performance, the ability to use the grammatical rules of language versus what is actually produced in speech. Almost as soon as Chomsky had introduced the distinction, scholars who studied the interaction between language and society noted that *competence* in Chomsky's sense left out a large amount of the knowledge needed to actually speak a language. Language is more than grammatical rules, after all. To speak a language, people need to know the rules of conversation, how to address other people appropriately, what to say when they see their neighbor in the morning, and so on. Hymes (1974) labeled this ability **communicative competence**. This chapter is concerned with various components of communicative competence, the rules for speaking appropriately in a given culture. The branch of linguistics that studies language in context is called **pragmatics**. The topics in this chapter are concerned with the pragmatic use of language.

Backchannels

Think for a moment about what your listeners are doing while you are talking with them. Oftentimes, they are making short sounds such as *uh huh, yeah, right.* These cues are called **backchannels,** and they are typically used by listeners to show that they are indeed listening to you and following your conversation. We learn these cues early on and tend to use them without even giving them much thought, usually during slight pauses in conversations. Think back on a recent telephone conversation you may have had. When the person on the other end doesn't provide these backchannel cues to indicate that he or she is listening, we often say, *Are you there?* The silence on the other end is not something we are accustomed to, and without these cues, we typically check in on the listener to actually see if he or she is still there (and awake!).

As you might have already guessed, backchannel cues vary across cultures. Not only are the sounds themselves different, but the meaning they carry may also be slightly different as well. What happens, then, when we are conversing with a person whose first language is not similar to our own? If your first answer was that some form of miscommunication might occur, you could quite possibly be right. Our first mistake as speakers is to assume that these cues represent some form of understanding on the part of our listener. This interpretation is tricky, as this could actually be true in some cases. However, these cues are often ambiguous and do not always convey understanding. Most often, these cues are seen as *continuers;* that is, they simply function to keep the conversation going. Learners pick up these cues quickly and begin using them early on when learning a new language in the country where it is spoken. If you are in regular contact with nonnative speakers of your own language, you will notice that the major contribution of the nonnative speaker during your conversations might be backchannel cues (or even simpler, head nods and smiles). These cues are easy to formulate and make the listener feel like they are a part of the conversation. What you can see from the very typical native speaker–nonnative speaker (NS-NNS) exchange in the following example is that the nonnative speaker is using plenty of backchannel cues but has very little understanding about what the speaker is saying. The cues are helping to keep the conversation going, but in no way can we use the backchannel cues as a way to know if the listener understands what the native speaker is saying. Here is a typical NS-NNS interaction, with several backchannels:

NS: This teacher is really interesting.
NNS: Uhuh.
NS: She gives us the best examples in class.
NNS: Mm-hmm.
NS: What do you think of her?
NNS: Pardon?
NS: Do you like the teacher?
NNS: Yes.

Varonis and Gass (1985) found that NNSs contributed mostly backchannel cues to a conversation, as is illustrated with the preceding NS-NNS exchange. They determined that NNSs' rampant use of backchannels led NSs to extend their end of the conversation, creating even more opportunities for miscommunication. Once learners reach more native-like fluency, this tendency may decrease. However, this is a constant danger to understanding, even at upper levels.

As we've noted, backchannel cues can be quite specific to each culture. In Japan, for example, backchannels or *aizuchi* are commonly found in conversation. What you will hear in Japanese, with great frequency, are *un* (yeah), *hai* (yes), and *soo* (is that right?). These backchannels in Japanese are most frequently used when seeking agreement from the listener and during topic changes. These small and seemingly insignificant aspects of language play a very important role in the Japanese language. Japanese may use up to three times more backchannels than their English-speaking counterparts. In one 35-minute study, more than 600 *aizuchi* were found. The notion that the Japanese take the listener's needs into account more than English speakers seem to may account for their high use of backchannels, as these are the cues that show involvement within a conversation.

Yamada's 1992 study showed that when Japanese and Americans conversed in business settings, the Japanese used more backchannels than the Americans—in both languages. This could be because the Japanese make a critical distinction between insiders and outsiders (e.g., those within and outside their company), and they may feel the need to smooth out and to help with conversations when conversing with outsiders. Boxer (1993) noted that English speakers found the Japanese use of backchannels to be excessive and that the English speakers in Japanese-English dyads (pairs) formed negative opinions about their Japanese conversation partner based on their interpretation that these cues were overused. It seemed to the English speakers that the Japanese were not adding critical content to the conversation and were simply agreeing with everything. As we have mentioned earlier, the use of backchannels does not necessarily signify agreement but could show simply that the listener is following the conversation—and even that can be deceiving. We see clearly the potential for miscommunication here and, on a greater scale, how stereotypes may be reinforced.

Related to backchanneling are the notions of overlap and interruption. *Overlap* is defined as two speakers talking at once in a facilitating way that contributes to the conversation. *Interrupting* occurs when one speaker talks on top of another in a way that harms the flow of the conversation.

Forms of Address

Social situations determine to a large degree how we address each other. When people are introduced in a professional or business situation in the United States, they frequently first address each other as Ms. Smith and Dr. Jones, using what linguists call TLN (title, last name). At some point, perhaps in that conversation or perhaps in the future, one of the speakers may suggest that the other give up TLN and use the first name (FN): *Call me Fred*. Which of the speakers does this has everything to do with issues of power (based on age, position, occupation, and gender). A professor is more likely to ask students to disregard her title and call her by her first name than vice versa; indeed, the professor may already have presumed upon her position and addressed the students by their first names without having been explicitly told to do so. It may be unthinkable in the context of a particular department for students to initiate an FN form of address with the faculty (and in another it may be just as unthinkable to use TLN). In an informal situation, people of the same age, especially younger people, may begin the interaction on an FN basis. This is an aspect of language that has changed significantly in the last 30 years in the United States and Europe, with the trend toward more informal address systems. We do tend to keep a certain distance with some people, however. You probably address your doctor as TLN, for example; this is an aspect of the power relationship between doctor and patient.

Brown and Gilman (1972) authored the classic study of address forms, which is based on European languages. Brown and Gilman distinguished *T* pronouns from *V* pronouns. The labels come from the fact that Latin had two pronouns, *tu* (originally singular *you*) and *vos* (originally plural *you*). These developed into the Spanish *tu/usted* and the French *tu/vous*. German has *du* and *Sie*. If you've studied any of these languages, you think of *T* pronouns as informal and *V* pronouns as formal. That is not all there is to it, however. In medieval Europe, people from the same class used reciprocal pronouns. Thus, equals of the upper class used *V* with each other, and equals of the lower class used *T*. When members of the upper class addressed members of the lower class, they used *T* and received *V* in return. Families also used this pattern, with parents being addressed by children with *V* and children being addressed by parents with *T*. This pattern was the norm well into the 19th century.

In the 20th century, there was a conscious move toward equality, or at least the appearance of it, in speech. Paulston (1976) captured an address system in flux in Sweden. The social democratic ethos of the country supported a change from the dual *T/V* system to a system of *T* alone, but Paulston notes that the wishes of society were mitigated by factors of long standing, including the social class system. Nevertheless, she was able to show that there were rules operating in a system the Swedes themselves saw as random.

Also in the 20th century, Chinese terms of address underwent significant change. Traditional Chinese terms of address were complex. There were different terms for older and younger sisters and for mother's brother and father's brother, for example. A guiding principle of the address system was respect for the elders; a young person addressing someone of the parents' generation would use the Chinese terms for *uncle* and *aunt*, for example. The establishment of the People's Republic of China led to the widespread use of *tongzhi* or *comrade*, which has, since the rise of the economic reforms of the 1990s, decreased in use. Traditional forms equivalent to *Mr., Mrs.,* and *Ms.* have been revived. Occupational forms of address such as *Master Worker* (*shifu*) and *boss* (*laoban*) are also now frequently used in the 2000s in China.

Japan has a traditional address system that shows no signs of disappearing. It is part of an extremely complex system of honorifics that we cannot lay out completely here. We will mention that Japanese has three common levels of markers for what in English would be *Mr.* and *Ms.* Only one level is marked for gender. At the highest level is *sama*, which gets attached to last names. *Tanaka-sama* is either Mr. or Ms. Tanaka, treated with a great deal of respect and social elevation. Everyday usage is marked by *san*. *Tanaka-san* refers to Mr. or Ms. Tanaka, with due respect, but with Tanaka not elevated above the speaker. *San* can also be used with first names, though in general Japanese use first names less than Americans do. More informal are *chan* (female) and *kun* (male). *Chan* and *kun* are frequently used with first names (Ai-*chan*, Ken-*kun*), particularly with young children, though *kun* can be used with last names and is so used in business situations when older colleagues are addressing younger ones (both male and female) familiarly.

With all this variation in address systems across languages, students in second language classrooms may be confused. In college classrooms in south Florida, where ESL classrooms are heavily populated with Haitian students, we have noticed an interesting example of intercultural miscommunication. We found that in Haitian Creole it is common to address your instructor as *Professeur*. This is typically transferred directly into the second language, in this case, English. Therefore, instead of addressing their teachers by TFN or FN, the students (and indeed, students of many cultures) simply raise their hand and call out *Teacher* during the middle of class time as an attention getter. These students may also use *Teacher* in face-to-face communication when alone with the instructor. This seemed to be discomforting for many mainstream (i.e., non-ESL) instructors at the college. These instructors often complained that their Haitian students were acting like kindergarten children as this is, for the most part, the only grade in the U.S. educational system in which the students are indeed allowed to address their teachers as *Teacher*. Even after multiple attempts at trying to explain this to the instructors and students on this particular campus, the frustration level did not lower for either of them. In the students' minds, they were addressing someone of higher status using the respectful term *Teacher* and could not see why there was a problem with this. This goes to show us that what is often embedded in our culture, and what may seem perfectly natural and respectful to us, may not be interpreted as appreciative by the listener (in this case, the teacher). Having said this, we must also remember from earlier in this chapter that some individuals, most notably medical doctors in the United States, are frequently addressed by their professional titles alone.

Contextualization Cues

By now, you are probably well aware that speakers have many ways of conveying meaning to their listeners. In addition to backchannel cues and forms of address, another such way is through **contextualization cues**. These cues help us better understand what we mean by what we say. These cues may come in the form of intonation, word choice, or pauses, to name a few. As native speakers of a language, for example, we usually know when someone is being sarcastic with us because of a change in intonation. Often this is a flat, monotone intonation pattern as seen in Nelms (2002). When cultures do not share the understanding of various contextualization cues, misunderstandings can occur. Think about the difficulties one might encounter when using humor or sarcasm in a second language. Although multiple factors are at play here and result in various interpretations of the utterance by NSs and NNSs, the lack of a shared understanding of contextualization cues is key. With multiple aspects of the second language to attend to simultaneously, it seems apparent that these subtle cues go unnoticed and cause problems for NNS listeners.

Another example of contextualization cues at work can be illustrated using word stress. If we hear a teacher in the next room say to a student "Sit down," this might be interpreted as the first attempt to get the student to do so. If, however, the teacher says, "I said, SIT DOWN," we might infer that the student has been told to do so on at least one other occasion and that the teacher is getting angry. Contextualization cues are key elements in all conversations because the speaker's every choice in performing or wording an utterance can make a difference in how that utterance is interpreted.

Children bring their own set of contextualization cues to the classroom with them, and these cues are often different from the ones that their teacher possesses. An oft-cited example is with Native American children who seem shy and perhaps uninterested in the teacher's lesson. This misinterpretation on the part of the teacher could be due largely to the fact that silence is more common in Native American conversation than it is in English-speaking cultures.

Gumperz's (1982) work with Indian and British English speakers shows clear evidence of the importance of contextualization cues. He shares multiple dialogues from a large study in which it is clear that the two groups are miscommunicating because of a lack of shared knowledge regarding contextualization cues. These differences in interpretations include various understandings of the way stress and intonation are used as well as pauses.

Speech Acts

Sometimes the intended meaning of an utterance is initially unclear but becomes clearer over time. Think about the following real-life example, which occurred when a college professor was returning his students' work. One of his students had miserably failed the assignment, and the professor said, "brilliant work," to the student as he handed back the paper. The student looked surprised, probably recalling that he thought he had not done well on this particular assignment. Then, as he saw his grade, he suddenly realized that the professor was being sarcastic and that the literal meaning was quite different from the intended meaning. We all know that failing an assignment does not illustrate brilliance. As listeners, we have to reconstruct these nonliteral, or implied, meanings from our shared knowledge about the world and the language that we speak. This is one of the main reasons why sarcasm is so difficult to understand in a second language. Even if our actual language abilities are quite strong in the second language, we often cannot interpret the utterance as sarcastic because we lack the shared world knowledge of the other culture. In determining how people understand the intended meaning of an utterance, we have to also understand how people use words. For this, we turn to the work philosophers J. L. Austin (1962/1975) and John Searle (1969) have done on speech act theory.

A **speech act** is any utterance produced by a speaker. Speech act theory is fundamentally interested in distinguishing three different acts in each utterance. The three are:

- **locutionary act**: the actual words spoken
- **illocutionary act**: the intention behind the words spoken
- **perlocutionary act**: the effect the words have on our hearers

To illustrate these three acts, we can think of the following classroom example. During an exam, a teacher says to the class "Eyes on your own paper" (locution), meaning, *Stop cheating!* (illocution); the perlocutionary effect might be that the students in question start doing their own work. As we can see, these interpretations are highly culturally specific. The intended meaning in the above utterance would be easy to derive by any native speaker of English who has attended schools in the United States. The utterance might be more difficult to interpret for a NNS who is new to the U.S., as is often the case with any utterance that does not have a clear intended meaning. When teaching NNSs then, we should try to always be aware of the intentions that we want our students to understand as the NNSs may not be interpreting them in the way we think that they are. An example of NNS-NS miscommunication that we have seen is when a teacher has announced to the class, "It sure is getting noisy in here," meaning *Be quiet!* In this situation, the NSs started to quiet down, but two NNSs interpreted this as a literal, descriptive comment by the teacher and made no efforts to be any quieter. This caused frustration on the part of the teacher, and at the same time, the NNSs were completely confused by what had just happened.

Another issue concerning these acts is that the same locution can have multiple interpretations. Think, for example, about the last time someone asked you what time it was. Did the speaker want to know the exact time? Was the speaker upset with you because you were late? Or did the speaker think it was time for you to go home? All of these are valid interpretations, depending on the situation, which can be all the more confusing for our NNS students.

Another way of addressing this issue is to say that the same utterance may fulfill different categories of speech act. Speech acts have five separate categorizations.

- *Representatives:* assertions, claims, and reports . . .
- *Directives:* requests, suggestions, commands . . .
- *Expressives:* thanks, apologies, complaints . . .
- *Commisives:* promises, refusals
- *Declaratives:* performatives (e.g., the act of making an utterance actually performs the act, as in "Class dismissed" or "I now pronounce you husband and wife")

Thus, "What time is it?" meaning *I don't have a watch and I'd like to know the time* can be categorized as a request or directive. When it means *You're late,* it is a complaint or expressive.

We can see that the most interesting aspect for intercultural communication is the illocutionary act. Much research has been done recently on a small handful of speech acts (e.g., apologies, compliments, complaints, requests), and we will share a few of these studies with you in Chapter 8.

Speech Events

Hymes (1972/1986) offers another approach to what he calls **speech events**. A conversation at a party or a discussion during a teacher's office hours would be two clear examples of a speech event. Hymes created the following mnemonic device for describing context.

> (**S**)ituation/(**S**)cene: a physical setting (e.g., the classroom) or an abstract setting (e.g., a committee meeting)
> (**P**)articipants: the speaker, hearer, audience, etc.
> (**E**)nds: the outcomes, purposes or goals (e.g., a verdict in a court case)
> (**A**)ct sequences: the content of the message; the form of the message
> (**K**)ey: the tone or manner (e.g., serious, sarcastic)
> (**I**)nstrumentals: the channel or mode (e.g., spoken, written; verbal or nonverbal); the form of speech (e.g., the accent or dialect a speaker chooses to use)
> (**N**)orms: the norms of interpretation or interaction within a cultural belief system
> (**G**)enre: textual categories (e.g., a joke, a lecture, etc.)

Now, let's apply Hymes's speaking grid to a traditional ten-minute ESL lecture to see how it might play out:

> (**S**)ituation/(**S**)cene: the classroom
> (**P**)articipants: instructor/students
> (**E**)nds: for students to learn the past tense
> (**A**)ct sequences: the lesson plan
> (**K**)ey: serious tone
> (**I**)nstrumentals: verbal/Standard English
> (**N**)orms: instructor talks/students listen
> (**G**)enre: lecture

One concern with Hymes's grid is that it does not allow for individual contributions to the speech event. That is, two students involved in the same situation (e.g., negotiating for a higher grade from a teacher during her office hours) often come out of the situation with different experiences (e.g., one is granted the higher grade, while the other is denied the higher grade). The linguistic situation could be exactly the same, thus not allowing Hymes's speaking grid to account for different individual outcomes when all other things are equal.

Another concern with Hymes's grid is that he was thinking of rather formal, often ritualized events, such as weddings or funerals, when he created it. We find it difficult to use this grid, for example, to describe casual conversations or other types of informal speech events.

Conversational Implicature

Working out implicated meaning can be tricky. How do we recover these implicitly communicated ideas? The most influential treatment of this phenomenon was done by Paul Grice (1975). He claims that people follow what he calls the **co-operative principle (CP)**, which is a set of norms and principles that guide communicative behavior. Grice assumes that the speaker follows the following four maxims in order to satisfy the co-operative principle:

Quality: Do not say what you believe to be false.
            Do not say that for which you lack adequate evidence.

Quantity: Make your contribution to the conversational
              exchange as informative as required.
            Do not make your contribution to the conversational
              exchange more informative than is required.

Relation: Be relevant.

Manner: Be brief.
            Be orderly.
            Avoid ambiguity.
            Avoid obscurity of expression.

When speakers blatantly fail to observe one of the previous maxims, they are said to be *flouting a maxim*. This inherently involves the generation of an *implicature* (an implied meaning). We can see that these four maxims can easily be intertwined, making it difficult to determine when one specific maxim is being flouted. For example, in one single utterance, a student might give a lengthy explanation (a flout of the maxim of manner, i.e., be brief) while telling a lie (a flout of the maxim of quality, i.e., do not say what you believe to be false) when trying to explain why he was late for class.

While there are multiple ways to fail to observe a maxim, we will discuss only one more with you. This is the notion of *infringing a maxim,* or unintentionally failing to observe a maxim. As we will see, this is crucial for those who work with international students to understand. In the case of NNSs of a language, the speaker may have no intention of generating an implicature and no intention at all of deceiving the hearer but still fail to observe a maxim. How can this happen? Most likely the failure to observe a maxim at this point is explained by imperfect linguistic performance rather than any attempt on the part of the speaker to deceive or to generate an implicature. This explains why we might witness this with international students, with children in their first language, or when a speaker's performance is impaired in some way (e.g., by being nervous or excited).

There are some apparent problems with Grice's theories. One major issue is that Grice expressed the CP in the imperative mood (as commands), so many people have interpreted this to mean that Grice was telling speakers how they should indeed behave. What he was actually saying was that when two people are conversing, they are working under a set of rules that guide their interaction in order to make it a smooth one—unless they have evidence to the contrary (e.g., a blatant lie).

Politeness

Another aspect of pragmatics that deserves attention is the notion of politeness. Brown and Levinson (1987) defined politeness as the way we show awareness of someone else's public self-image or **face**. Face can be divided into **positive face**—or a person's need to be liked and respected, to be considered a member of a group—and **negative face**—or a person's desire to be left alone, to not be put upon by others.

If you say something that represents a threat to another person's face, you commit a *face-threatening act.* There are a number of ways to soften the threat. You might adopt a *politeness strategy* such as apologizing in advance ("I'm sorry to bother you, but could I ask you for a favor?") or drawing the hearer into your situation ("Could you do me a favor and loan me a dollar?").

How do we know how severe a face-threatening act is? Brown and Levinson say that we must take into account the power relationship between the speaker and hearer (Is one the boss?), the social distance between the two (Are they friends?), and the degree of imposition involved (People more readily loan pens than cars.).

All of these factors are of course defined culturally. Brown and Levinson acknowledge that different cultures manifest politeness in different ways, but they claim that the basic principle of their model of politeness, the human desire for face, is universal. However, because their notion of face depends on the notion of self and because the idea of what constitutes the "self" is itself cultural, other scholars have seen the model as inherently Western.

Teaching Scenarios

1. A teacher is told by a parent, "Please do your best to help my son." The teacher is offended by the thought she would do anything less than her best. Based on your knowledge of speech acts from this chapter, what do you think is going on here? What is happening in terms of politeness?

2. You are from a small town in the Midwestern United States, and you are having a casual conversation with a friend from a large city in the Northeast. Every time you say something, she seems to cut you off and add something to the conversation. You feel frustrated. Later, your friend talks to a mutual friend of yours, and she complains that you just don't ever seem interested in her and what she has to say. What could be happening?

☑ Check Your Knowledge

1. Define communicative competence.
2. Give examples of backchannels. What is the purpose of backchanneling?
3. How do forms of address change across cultures? Give some examples.
4. What are contextualization cues, and what part do they play in intercultural misunderstanding?
5. What are speech acts? What are locutionary, illocutionary, and perlocutionary acts?
6. Why is it useful to categorize speech acts into categories such as representatives, directives, etc?
7. What is the co-operative principle (CP)? What maxims satisfy the CP?
8. Briefly sketch Brown and Levinson's theory of politeness.

Apply Your Knowledge

1. Tape-record a five-minute casual conversation with a friend. Count the number of backchannels that are used, and make a list of the various ones you find. Compare and discuss the frequency and types in class.
2. Look back at the sentences in 3 in the Before You Read box. For each situation you thought of, give the locutionary act, illocutionary act, and perlocutionary act. Are there cases in which intercultural misunderstandings might arise?
3. Think of misunderstandings involving contextualization cues you have experienced.
4. Analyze a conversation in a film or TV show for use of the co-operative principle. Where in the conversation is the CP followed, and where is it not observed?
5. Watch a movie or TV show and apply Brown and Levinson's theory of politeness to some of the conversations in it.

Reflect

How real are these "rules" for conversation? Think about your own conversational practice in light of the ideas in this chapter.

Expand Your Knowledge

1. 🎬 Watch the film *Crosstalk*. Pay particularly close attention to the scene involving a British headmaster and an Indian student's father. See if you can determine the sources of miscommunication between the two individuals. How could both participants in the conversation change in order to achieve more successful interactions in the future? Note that this film is typically not available in video stores, but is very easy to get through interlibrary loan. It is also available through the Center for Media and Independent Learning, Berkeley, California (cmil@uclink.berkeley.edu).

2. Find people who speak another language. Ask them to have a conversation in their native language, and try to pick out the backchannels without understanding the conversation.

3. Read Gumperz (1982). Look at the dialogues and report on the specific problems encountered.

4. If you are interested in philosophy, you might want to read all or part of Austin (1962/1975).

5. Find out about other theories of politeness besides Brown and Levinson. A good place to start would be an encyclopedia of linguistics. Write a short report on your findings.

Suggested Readings

James Paul Gee. *An Introduction to Discourse Analysis: Theory and Method*. New York: Routledge, 1999.

Numa Markee. *Conversation Analysis*. Mahwah, NJ: Lawrence Erlbaum Associates, 2000.

Deborah Tannen. *Gender and Discourse*. New York: Ballantine, 1999.

First Language Acquisition, Individual Bilingualism, and the Schools

5

1. Think of words you use with infants. How are they different from words that you use with adults?

2. What do you know about your experience learning your first language? Did people correct your grammar mistakes? Your pronunciation? Was there any sort of formal instruction involved before you entered school?

3. ⊞ List things people do to help babies learn their first language or culture. What is each thing good for?

Chapter 5 will help you understand the processes of first language and bilingual acquisition as well as the process of socialization (or becoming a member of a culture). We then apply this knowledge of language acquisition and socialization to what happens when children go to school and show how differences in culture may lead to unequal educational opportunities. The chapter also relates the knowledge of bilingual acquisition to the forms bilingual programs take.

This chapter surveys first language acquisition, the acquisition of two or more languages simultaneously in childhood (bilingualism), and children's experiences in schools. Chapter 6 will focus on the acquisition of second languages and cultures by both children and adults.

Learning a First Language

We noted in Chapter 2 that linguists consider language to be biological. The biological *ability* to acquire language needs to be set into motion through interacting with caregivers. Interaction is key to learning a first language. People seem to know instinctively how to talk to babies. This **child-directed speech (CDS),** also called caregiver speech or "motherese," seems to provide the sort of input that is good for language acquisition. CDS is characterized in middle-class Western cultures by a slower rate of speech; a higher pitch; varied or singsong intonation; a lot of pausing; short, simple sentences; frequent repetition and paraphrase; questioning; and a focus on the here-and-now (what is immediately in front of the child and interlocutor). The purpose of CDS seems to be to break speech up into understandable units. Think of when you first learned a foreign language. The sounds all rushed by you in an undifferentiated mass. You probably could not tell where one word ended and another began. If your teacher spoke slowly in short sentences, you gradually got the meaning. The high, musical pitch of CDS might be an attention-getting device used to clue the baby to important parts of the sentence. All of the characteristics of caregiver speech serve not to teach language, however. In that regard, our analogy to foreign language learning in school is a bad one. Parents do not teach language; they facilitate its acquisition. CDS serves to facilitate communication and thereby acquisition. Because the focus is on communication, parents do not always correct the child's mistakes, though if there is just one mistake they may focus on it more than they would if the child's utterance contained several errors. Still, the parents are not likely to offer a grammatical rule or a direct correction of the mistake. They are much more likely to simply repeat the error or ask a question to clarify something they don't understand. Older siblings and, in some research at least, fathers may push the child toward clarity more than mothers may. Older (school-age) siblings in general are less patient interlocutors than parents; they engage in less CDS, drop conversations when they don't understand the younger child, and usually are more demanding conversational partners. This may lead to conversational breakdown, but it may also be useful for acquisition.

CDS differs across cultures. In Qu'iche (Central America), higher-pitched speech is a mark of respect accorded to people of higher status and therefore is inappropriate for children; caregivers whisper instead. Tonal languages such as Chinese or Thai generally do not elevate pitch; in these languages, rising and falling tones are used to differentiate words. (So, in Chinese, *ma* said with different tones means "mother" or "horse.") Among the Kaluli (Papua New Guinea), nonsense syllables are associated with the souls of dead children; baby talk is not used among the living. Still, some degree of simplification and exaggeration is found in speech to children throughout the world. What differs is a matter of degree or frequency. Some cultures, such as the Javanese (Indonesia) and Western Samoans (southern Pacific), tend not to simplify but use repetition instead. In many cultures, it is the task of the child to accommodate the adults; children are "seen and not heard" and their conversational initiatives are not responded to (Schieffelin and Ochs 1986; Rogoff 2003). We will have more to say about appropriateness in language in Chapter 6. First, we will briefly outline the first two years of language acquisition. In doing so, we will use averages. Some children will progress at a slower rate, but all children go through the same basic stages.

Children are born with an ability to discriminate sounds not found in their own language. To find this out, researchers typically play a recording of a sound being repeated; when the phoneme changes, the child being tested is likely to notice the change and show that either by turning the head or by otherwise changing behavior. Children notice the change even if they haven't heard that sound produced in the language they hear daily. For instance, children of Canadian English speakers were able to distinguish two consonants in Salish (western North America) and two in Hindi (India), even though their parents could not do so. That is, while parents could not tell when the sound changed, infants could. Children lose this ability by the age of ten months to one year (Werker and Tees 1984).

Children at first produce similar sounds across languages. For the first three months, babies have the ability to cry, laugh, and produce what are called vegetative sounds (burps, sneezes, coughs). It usually takes at least two months before the parents can differentiate crying so that they can tell a request for attention from a call for relief of discomfort. Around four months, babbling begins, with the repetition of individual vowel or consonant sounds. Babbling continues as sounds are added together (*bababa*). Most babbling sounds the same across languages. Only when adults hear longer stretches of sound can they reliably say which language is being babbled; they seem to be able to do this mostly because of intonational cues. For example, adults in a study by Boysson-Bardies, Sagart, and Durand (1984) were able to tell which babies were speaking Cantonese, Arabic, and French based on prosodic cues.

There is no exact line between babbling and speech. Words come out of babbling, and the practice of babbling continues as the child adds new words. First words are often conventionalized in a culture. To be sure, most cultures believe a baby's first word is *mama*, but some cultures in the western Pacific believe that the first word is a cry of independence, either a rude remark or something like, *"I'm getting out of here."* Once words begin, they slowly accumulate. Children produce their first word between the age of nine months and a year, have about 10 words at 15 months old, and about 50 at 20 months. They may well understand, but not be able to produce, 50 words much earlier, around 13 months. As children acquire new words and new structures, they have a tendency to overgeneralize their meanings, so that *dog* may mean any animal, not just the family pet. A *ball* may be anything round.

Boysson-Bardies and her colleagues (1999) found an overlap of about 12 percent in production of first words among French, Swedish, American, and Japanese infants. Children in all four countries talked about mommy, daddy, baby, eyes, shoes, ball, peek-a-boo, no, and good-bye. All the children produced a lot of nouns. In an almost comical reinforcement of our stereotypes, French babies talked more about food and clothing; Swedish infants used comparatively more verbs and liked to name household objects such as lamps and clocks; American children used the fewest number of verbs, preferring to name objects around them, and they used a lot of greetings; Japanese babies made frequent use of social formulas for hello, good-bye, and thank you.

As children are learning new words, they are also learning the morphology and syntax of their language. In the middle of their second year, children move into the *two-word stage*. English-speaking children say things such as *more juice, more car,* and *more cereal* or *all gone* and *all wet*. A French-speaking child might say things such as *encore de l'eau, donne l'eau,* and *canard dans l'eau (more water, give water, duck in the water)* (Boysson-Bardies 1999). These sort of utterances are truly creative. The child would not have heard an adult saying them. The utterances are simple but systematic. They follow rules of the native language, such as adjective before noun in English. Some topics are very important for this age group: possession (*my dolly*), location (*dolly bed*), recurrence (*more juice*), and relationships (*bye bye daddy*) are all things children like to talk about in the two-word stage.

Piaget claimed that a child first learned a concept and then the word for it. Most of the research in child language development has followed this model. Recent research has claimed, however, that things are not this simple: language has an influence on semantic development. Bowerman and Choi (2001), for example, showed how English and Korean children are sensitive to their respective spatial systems at an early age. While English has *in*, Korean distinguishes tight and loose fits, so to put a piece in a jigsaw puzzle is described by the Korean verb *kkita* and to put a toy in a box is *nehta*. While all children have life experience of the concept of enclosure, that concept is filtered through the native language.

At the age of two, children are on the verge of acquiring many of the grammatical concepts of their respective languages. They will soon expand beyond the two-word stage and start producing more adult-like utterances. This does not all happen at once, of course. Children go through many stages of learning. What is interesting is that children learning a particular language will go through the same stages. Children learning different languages will follow certain universals. For example, no matter the words used to express the concepts, more concrete question words tend to be acquired before less concrete. In English, that means that children tend to acquire *what* and *who* before they acquire *why* and *how*. The first set is relatively concrete, the second relatively abstract. Similarly, across languages, children tend to acquire *in, on,* and *under* before they acquire *between*, because the relative relationships expressed are easier in the first case.

Children develop an increasingly better control over their language throughout childhood. A proper understanding of the passive voice (e.g., the difference between *The girl is kissed by the doll* and *The doll is kissed by the girl*) tends to be acquired relatively late, and younger children may not be able to correctly show the action of these kinds of sentences when they hear them spoken by researchers. However, most children have a very good grasp of their language before they enter kindergarten; the purpose of school is to teach literacy and formal rules of language, not to teach language itself.

Bilingual Language Acquisition

What of the child who learns two languages? Researchers distinguish **simultaneous bilingualism** from sequential or successive bilingualism. Simultaneous bilinguals learn two languages from birth, most often as a result of parents speaking two different languages. In some cases, a child may learn first one language and then another. When this happens after the age of three, it is termed **sequential bilingualism**.

Simultaneous bilinguals follow the same pattern of acquisition as monolingual children. Their progress in learning both languages may be somewhat slower than the progress of monolinguals (after all, they are learning twice as much). At first, the bilingual child may have one word for each object or action in the environment. A Spanish-English bilingual may refer to a dog as *perro* and a doll as *doll*. This leads to a kind of intrasentence mixing of languages. By the age of three, certainly, and in some cases perhaps as early as two, bilingual children sort the two languages apart, and they reach the same level of linguistic development as their monolingual peers by the age of four or five. Experts recommend that in the case of parents having separate languages, a policy of one parent–one language be adopted to facilitate acquisition. This may lead in some cases to overgeneralization. All men may be spoken to "in daddy's language" and all women "in mommy's language."

Bilingual children frequently keep their languages separate by imposing boundaries by person (speaking to grandparents in one language, friends in another) or domain (speaking one language in school, another at home).

Learning a First Culture

Socialization is the term for the process by which individuals learn how to be a member of a given culture. Culture and language are intertwined in this process; the child learns cultural information through language but also learns how to speak—in many different ways—within the culture. Children learn different *registers* (formal and informal) of language as well as different *lects* (social and regional dialects, for example). They learn when it is appropriate to use one variety of the language and when another is better suited to circumstances. They learn how to speak like women or men, how to tell stories, and what to think about the various ways of speaking, for all cultures assign value to certain lects over others. They do all of this through interaction with more experienced members of the culture. It is not only children who are socialized, of course; adults are socialized as well. (See Bayley and Schecter 2003 for a wider perspective.)

Humans are in some sense born to communicate. Most children prefer faces early on, before they begin to babble. Children seek out contact with others. Eye contact is initiated by the child at about four weeks of age. Gradually, accompanied with gestures and vocalizations, eye contact leads to play, which leads to communication between parent and child. Consider peek-a-boo. Games like this model interaction. At first, the child may be invited into the game through rising intonation. Gradually, the child learns to take turns hiding eyes and may even initiate the game. Another form of parent/child interaction is turn-taking with vocalizations, where the baby echoes the parent. Still another happens when the parent points and names something. As the child gets older and the parent begins to read picture books, in U.S. middle-class culture there is a routine that consists of getting the child's attention (*Look!*), asking a question (*What's this?*), getting feedback from the child (*da*), and evaluation from the parent (*Yes, a doggy!*). All of these behaviors model the back and forth of adult conversation that the child must learn. However, the child is not just passing information back and forth to the caregiver; much of the purpose of the interaction is establishing a relationship, drawing the other person in.

All cultures are quite concerned with how to teach children to be members of society. This is often done quite explicitly in U.S. culture: "Stop acting like a baby." "Big boys don't do that." There are of course intercultural differences in parent/child interaction. While American middle-class parents are concerned to have their children name things in a picture book, Japanese parents put themselves in the position of the child during the reading of the book. They say things like, "Oh, what's this? This is so difficult—so many pictures. Now, where's the dog?" (Morikawa, Shand, and Kosawa 1988; Bornstein et al. 1992).

Even though Japanese mothers in particular strike American observers (such as us) as rather permissive, even indulgent, compared to American mothers, they are very concerned to instruct their children on how to act in a society that asserts an individual's responsibility to the group. (See also Tobin, Wu, and Davidson 1989.) Japanese mothers often use the strategy of imagining the reaction of others. Their response to bad behavior may be "people will laugh," or they may call the behavior strange or scary. They may say "no one does that" (Clancy 1986).

Some cultures, like the Kaluli (Papua New Guinea), direct their children's speech very overtly. The Kaluli mark the utterances they want the child to repeat with the phrase *elema* (say like that). They may use the phrase to initiate a game, to teach the child how to request something from older people, or to correct an utterance the child has already made. The Kaluli do not believe in baby talk, which they characterize as *soft*. They believe children should be encouraged to say *hard* language, and so they model adult speech for them to repeat (Schieffelin 1979).

Over the course of the first three years, children acquire the ability to perform most of the communicative acts appropriate to their culture. As Ninio and Snow (1996) detail, the communicative acts are acquired in an order from those that are highly contextualized, like peek-a-boo, to those that are relatively decontextualized and have little to do with the here and now, such as apologizing for something in the recent past or asking and answering *why* questions, which reference a reality that is not immediate.

As children grow older, they engage in conversations with people both inside and outside the family. Though they have been interacting since they were born, conversation is difficult to master. Whereas adults exchange turns relatively smoothly, children may remain silent if they are not sure what to say. At first, children have a hard time maintaining their turn to talk, since they speak slowly and sometimes not so fluently. By the age of four, however, children learn how to use devices such as *And* at the beginning of sentences to signal that they are not finished. It may take the child to the age of 12 to become adept at showing, through devices such as *so* and *anyway*, how one topic is connected to another. Young children may seem to bounce around a lot in their conversation because they frequently refer to events long past or outside their interlocutor's experience.

Classroom Language

Before beginning this section, we should remind ourselves of some of the caveats of Chapter 1. We noted there the widespread earlier belief in the deficit model, which took differences in culture to be deficits that needed to be remediated. We said that the deficit model was an example of *ethnocentrism*, the belief in the superiority of one's own group.

By the time children enter school, they are very competent users of their first language(s), though, as we have seen, they still have some things to learn about more advanced grammatical structures such as the passive or about how to converse more effectively. Once they enter school, children begin to work more intensively on what we have called **decontextualized language**. Indeed, you might say school is about decontextualized language. Children learn to appreciate stories about the past or about faraway places; they learn to write and speak in ways that effectively communicate the ideas and feelings inside them to other people who may not have the same ideas and feelings. In discussing the two registers that new speakers of a language must learn, Cummins (1989) distinguishes between the decontextualized language of the schools, or *CALP* (Cognitive Academic Language Proficiency), and the contextualized language of home and playground, or *BICS* (Basic Interpersonal Communication Skills). (See Solomon and Rhodes 1995 for a useful discussion of the issue of academic language in general.)

Sharing and *show and tell* are labels many schools give to the time when children may bring a possession or story to school and "share" it with others in a short oral presentation. In the early grades, sharing presents interesting issues for the teacher: Are the other kids getting bored? Do they understand what the speaker is saying? How much should I intervene in the story with questions and clarifications? Teachers differ in their approaches, but most seem to use the time to give students practice in communicating in ways they deem clear. Therein lies a problem. There have been numerous reports of intercultural misunderstandings during sharing, including between white teachers and African-American students. Cazden (2001), following the terminology of Smitherman (1986), talks about topic-centered and episodic approaches to narrative. Cazden says that the topic-centered approach, which generally addresses and expands on one story line, is preferred by the white school culture, whereas the episodic narrative style is favored by the African-American community. For example, African-American adults praised a sharing story told by a young African-American girl as being rich in detail and examples, while white adults criticized the same story as being disjointed (Cazden 2001).

Just as children learn to tell stories in the way sanctioned by the school culture, they also learn the characteristic discourse pattern of the school, what has been variously called the **IRE/IRF sequence**. In both cases, **I** stands for initiation and **R** for student response. **E** is for evaluation and **F** for feedback. Thus, in the following two cases, the teacher is evaluating the student response.

> *Teacher:* What's the capital of California?
> *Student:* Sacramento.
> *Teacher:* Good!

or

> *Teacher:* What did you do during the vacation?
> *Student:* We went to Disneyland.
> *Teacher:* That sounds like fun!

Conversations in North American schools characteristically have taken this form. To be sure, there have been attempts to break out of this pattern by teachers interested in getting their students to give longer and perhaps more thoughtful answers, but in many places the *recitation script* lives on and is one of the first things children must learn to be successful in school. It follows students from kindergarten through graduate school. It is part of the roles assigned teachers and learners. In most classrooms, the teacher decides who speaks and when (*Raise your hand!*). The teacher asks display questions, questions she already knows the answer to, in order to maintain the IRE sequence (*Good!*). In general, the rules of classroom discourse do not very closely mirror the rules of real world discourse.

However, some have pointed out that there is a difference between IRE and the IRF. When the teacher evaluates, the learning opportunity gets closed down. When the teacher instead gives feedback by following up the student utterance (*How did you get that answer?*) or extending the discussion (*Does anyone else have an idea?*), opportunities for deeper learning occur (Nassaji and Wells 2000).

Philips (1983) showed how the school culture of the Warm Springs Indian Reservation put its Native American students at a disadvantage in part because the students' discourse rules were different from those of the community. The school privileged auditory forms of learning at the expense of visual forms. Native American children are raised at home with a lot of face-to-face interaction and visual learning; ritualized activities are taught this way. Expectations of speech are also different. The young are seen and not heard. Among adults, value is placed on speech that is economical and controlled. The amount of backchannel behavior necessary to show that one is listening (*Um. Uh huh. Is that so?*) is less among the Warm Springs Indians than among the "Anglos" who live nearby. There are also differences in loudness and pace in conversation, with Native American speakers being softer in tone and allowing for longer pauses (Philips 1983).

Philips (1983) found that when the Warm Springs children go to school, their style of speaking bumps up against the school style. The Native American children talk less and respond less than the "Anglo" children, as is appropriate in their culture. They tend to ask more questions to make sure they understood; this is evaluated negatively by the teachers. These children's listening behavior is different too. They do not look at the teacher or give backchannel cues, again, as appropriate in their culture. They make fewer efforts to raise their hands to volunteer but also are more likely to talk (from the Anglo perspective) out of turn.

Philips interprets all this in light of culture. The Indian students, she says, are not used to speaking as a single person to a single adult authority figure. They do much better in small groups. The style of the classroom was not culturally appropriate to them. Given that Philips's research was done 30 years ago, we might question if the same problems are relevant today. Today, for example, there is an increased use of group work in classrooms. Tharp and Yamauchi (1994) suggest this research remains relevant. They review later studies of different groups of Native Americans and recommend what they call "culturally compatible education," including small-group work and practical activity in classrooms, to address lingering problems. (See also Osborne 1996 for a synthesis of ethnographic research on culturally appropriate pedagogy.)

In Hawaii, the Kamehameha Elementary Education Program (KEEP) was based on ideas of "assisted performance." Rather than following the IRE script, teachers drew out information in an "instructional conversation" format. In an effort to offer culturally appropriate instruction, teachers used the model of "talk story," an adult conversational style indigenous to Hawaiian culture that is characterized by frequent overlaps in speech, a sort of joint performance of the story (Tharp and Gallimore 1988).

Part of what KEEP addressed were issues of classroom control such as "talking out of turn"; culturally appropriate instruction solves many perceived discipline problems if children can work in structures they are familiar with from home life. The language of discipline itself may be different between home and school. Ballenger (1999) shows the differences not only in expectations of behavior (immigrant parents often think U.S. schools are not strict enough), but also the differences in ways children are reprimanded or otherwise controlled. She shows how her language in the classroom changed to fit the Haitian community's model of asking children rhetorical questions like *Do you kick at home?*

Delpit (1988) argues for explicit discussions of "the culture of power," the dominant culture of the school. She urges making the rules of school discourse explicit to students and asserts the value of teachers getting insights from parents about the sort of instruction that their children require. Delpit wants to honor the home culture, but also, in fairness, to make the rules and what is expected transparent so that students can be successful.

It is possible to push the cultural differences model too far as an explanation for educational problems. We need to acknowledge that many school districts are underfunded, that there are shortages of qualified teachers, and that society does not treat all groups equally. Losey (1997) gives examples of the cultural mismatches between teachers and students. She notes that teachers frequently interact differently with students from other cultures. For example, Anglo-American teachers of Mexican-American students have been shown to ask fewer questions of and to call on bilingual students less frequently, often with the seemingly benign motive of not wanting to draw attention to the students' (perceived) poor English ability. Losey also points out that schools exist within communities and that these communities often have a history of differential treatment of their citizens, in effect, in her word, "silencing" the less powerful voices. Padron,

Waxman, and Rivera (2002), in a synthesis of research on appropriate educational techniques for Hispanic students, endorse culturally responsive teaching but also cite the effectiveness of cooperative learning, reciprocal teaching, and technology-enhanced instruction.

Parental Involvement

Parental involvement is an important component of many school district plans. *Parental involvement* means different things to different people. Some researchers and policy makers speak of providing supportive home environments, having high expectations of student achievement, and undertaking joint participation in activities such as reading and storytelling as good forms of parental involvement. Others stress knowledge of what happens at school or parental participation at school.

Given economic realities, many parents simply cannot participate in school-based activities; they may be limited to home-based support. Second language learners may come from families for which certain forms of parental involvement are difficult. Parents may not speak the language of the school, for example, or may come from cultures where it is considered impolite, even presumptuous, for the parent to interfere with schooling because the teacher knows best. Some claim, for example, that Latin American cultures tend to believe that the school performs a different function from the family; the school educates and provides skills, while the family teaches morality and ethics. Schecter and Bayley's (2002) ethnography of Mexican-American families in Texas and California shows that, in fact, these families are quite involved with children's homework. In any case, the school can reach out to Latino families in a number of ways. Bilingual support is obviously critical for some families. Teachers can pay home visits to develop the necessary personal relationships and rapport with parents. Community outreach in the form of family literacy programs or ESL programs may be appropriate (Espinosa 1995).

One effective program to increase Pacific Islander parental involvement is the Hawaii Parent-Community Networking Center Program, which has established classrooms as meeting places for families, teachers, and community members. The centers are staffed part-time by facilitators who provide resources and referrals to community agencies. The purpose of the program is to develop a sense of community through networking homes and schools as well as to support student learning (Onikawa, Hammond, and Koki 1998).

Models of Bilingual Education

Before we sketch the forms bilingual education can take, we should note that across the United States bilingual education is under attack politically. Several states have held referendums calling for the ending of all bilingual education. Some have passed and others have failed, so the trend is not yet clear, and the issue promises to be with the nation for several years.

Bilingual education can take many forms. *Sheltered instruction* combines studying content such as science with supplementary materials geared specifically to English language learners. The teacher of the content area has expertise in second language learning and is able to present the material in a way that is comprehensible to students with intermediate language skills.

Newcomer programs meet the needs of immigrant students who have limited English proficiency; many of the students in these programs also have limited literacy skills in their first language as a result of limited or interrupted schooling. Some programs develop first language skills along with second language skills, while others focus on the second language and content knowledge.

Transitional or early-exit bilingual education is the most common form of bilingual education in the United States. Transitional bilingual education provides academic content instruction in the first language as learners acquire English. Thus, students do not fall behind in their subjects. In the beginning, many of these programs teach first language literacy skills as they simultaneously teach second language oral skills and content in classes where language is not the focus (e.g., music, art, physical education). Transitional bilingual education does not try to bring students to full bilingualism. It uses the first language to acquire the second.

Developmental or late-exit bilingual education aims to educate students in two languages. Academic content is taught in both languages for a number of years, typically as long as the school district has the resources, ideally through high school.

Two-way immersion classrooms are evenly divided between speakers of two languages. Both languages are used to teach academic content. The goal is to develop both languages, to foster what is called *additive bilingualism* (Genesee 1999).

Second language immersion focuses on students who speak the majority language (e.g., speakers of English in Canada). These programs use a second language (in the Canadian case, French) to teach content. This sort of program is also used to teach heritage languages such as Chinese in California or Hawaiian in Hawaii.

In the United States, a speaker of a heritage language is someone who was raised in an environment where a language other than English was spoken. The heritage language speaker may in fact be mostly a comprehender of the language rather than a speaker, but proficiencies vary widely. Some heritage language speakers are basically bilingual but may control only one register of the language; they may, for example, be able to engage in everyday conversation but have difficulty speaking appropriately in formal situations.

Historically, ethnic communities wishing to maintain their heritage languages have set up after-school or Saturday programs in community centers. Recently attempts have been made to encourage speakers of other languages to maintain them through heritage language programs. Secondary schools have played a small but important part in this movement. Programs in Spanish are the most highly developed, largely because the number of Spanish heritage language speakers is large compared to other languages; thus, it is possible to effectively group students and deliver instruction. In some high schools and universities, there are Spanish classes for native speakers of Spanish. These classes focus on the acquisition of a prestige variety of Spanish, on developing grammatical correctness, and on literacy. The overall goal is the maintenance of Spanish. Other languages, such as Arabic, Chinese, and Italian, are highlighted in certain regions of the United States (Peyton, Ranard, and McGinnis 2001).

In Japan, there are similar programs for returnee children. Japanese companies post large numbers of Japanese staff abroad. The children of the overseas staff must attend schools in the communities where their parents are posted. Though almost all Japanese companies help organize after-school and Saturday Japanese lessons to help the children maintain Japanese language and literacy skills, there is often some attrition of first language ability that accompanies sequential bilingualism. A number of specialized programs in Japan seek to make the reentry of the returnees smoother through instruction in language and literacy.

Teaching Scenarios

1. Children from a given culture are failing in their studies, and a large number of them are being placed in special education classes. These children seem not to listen when the teacher is talking. Instead, they whisper to their friends and seem to be bored. Could this situation have a cultural component? What would you need to know to be sure?

2. Parents approach the principal and complain that their children are playing games in English class. Indeed, the children are playing Bingo to review new words. What might be the roots of this parental dissatisfaction, and how should the principal deal with this complaint?

 Check Your Knowledge

1. What are the characteristics of Western middle-class child-directed speech?
2. Do parents *teach* language?
3. In what ways is first language acquisition universal? In what ways does culture play a role?
4. How does bilingual language acquisition differ from monolingual first language acquisition?
5. How do children learn to be conversation partners?
6. What are some ways home and school language may clash? Give examples.
7. How may expectations for parental involvement differ across cultures?
8. What are the models for bilingual education?

9. Be able to define these terms:

Child-directed speech

sequential/simultaneous bilingualism

socialization

decontextualized language

IRE/IRF sequence

heritage language

Apply Your Knowledge

1. How would the following change if you were speaking to an infant? What would the CDS versions of these statements be in your household?

    Mom/Dad

    water

    I wonder if you could pick up that toy?

    That's a really interesting item.

    You look exhausted.

2. ⊞ What are your impressions of school in your culture? First complete this questionnaire about elementary schools on your own. Along the line, mark where your own beliefs lie between the two statements. Is what you believe different from most people? Discuss the questionnaire in a group.

Individual development in school is most important.	Schools should develop the society, not individuals.
├─────────────────┤	

The most important thing for students to learn in school is to work independently.	The most important thing for students to learn in school is how to work in a group.
├─────────────────┤	

The purpose of schools is skill-getting.	The purpose of schools is socialization.
├─────────────────┤	

Students should be active in class.	Students should listen to the teacher.
The teacher should be an authority.	The teacher should be a guide to learning.
The role of parents is to teach students in the home.	Parents must be involved in the schools.

Reflect

1. Look back at question 2 in the Before You Read box. Can you recall any more experiences after having read this chapter? Is there anything in the chapter that does not match your personal experiences with first language learning?

Expand Your Knowledge

1. Visit a local school that has programs that you are interested in (e.g., bilingual education program, pre-K program, adult education, etc.). Observe a few classes, and focus on the way the teachers and students communicate. Note such things as
   - how often (and when) each language is spoken (where appropriate)
   - how directions are given
   - the amount of teacher and student talk
   - how new topics are introduced
   - how the students are put into groups
   - how students ask—and teachers respond—to questions
2. ▦ Watch the video *The Human Language Series Part 2, Acquiring the Human Language: Playing the Language Game* (Ways of Knowing Inc.). What other examples of first language acquisition does the video provide?

3. 🎬 Watch *Genie: Portrait of a Wildchild*. Write a report including any new information that you have acquired.

Suggested Readings

Joseph J. Tobin, David Y. H. Wu, and Daana H. Davidson. *Preschool in Three Cultures: Japan, China, and the United States*. New Haven, CT: Yale University Press, 1989.

Ana Maria Villegas and Tamara Lucas. *Educating Culturally Responsive Teachers: A Coherent Approach*. Albany: State University of New York Press, 2002.

The Diversity Kit: An Introductory Resource for Social Change in Education. www.alliance.brown.edu/tdl

Learning a Second Language

1. What stages have you gone through on your way to learning another language?

2. Why do you think learners make errors when trying to speak a second language?

3. ⊞ Think back to your own experiences learning another language. Describe the various activities your instructor used to teach pragmatic skills in the language classroom.

Chapter 6 will help you understand the process of second language acquisition. It will focus on what it means to know a second language. We also explore misunderstandings that arise from intercultural differences in language use and whether appropriate language use can be taught in second language classrooms.

Second Language Learning

It is conventional, if somewhat misleading, to refer to the acquisition of another language, after the first or native language **(L1)** has been acquired, as second language **(L2)** acquisition or SLA. Many people, of course, acquire more than two languages, and what we label as SLA may really be third or fourth language acquisition. In reality, not much research has been done on the differences between learning a second language and subsequent languages, so we will be silent on this point. Furthermore, we will be most concerned in this chapter with the *pragmatics* of additional language acquisition. However, before beginning that topic, we want to briefly outline SLA at a psycholinguistic level.

Scholars disagree about how second languages are learned and people certainly learn in different ways. Here we will present a basic introduction.

Second language acquisition occurs through at least two processes, the process of **transfer** and the process of *interlanguage*. Transfer refers to the fact that the first language may affect learning at all levels: sounds, grammar, words, and appropriacy. The clearest example is accent. Few people who learn a language in adulthood lose the way they pronounce sounds in L1. An English-speaking adult learning Spanish will have difficulty rolling the *r* sound where necessary. The same person learning French will have a hard time with the *r* sound in *rien*, which is made in the back of the throat. English has neither of these *r* sounds, so the learner uses (transfers) the English *r* instead. Another clear example is what is often called *false friends*. These are cognate words that look like they should be the same in both languages but are not. Consider the French word *information*, which means *news*, or the word *sensible*, which means *sensitive*. A classic example in Spanish is the word *embarazada*, which means *pregnant* (and not *embarrassed*, which can obviously get English speakers learning Spanish into trouble). While language learners are sometimes hindered by transfer, they may also be helped in those cases where the languages in fact are close at some point.

While the learner's first language has an effect on the acquisition of the second, it is also true that all learners, regardless of L1, go through similar processes. The most important is the **interlanguage (IL)** process. Interlanguage is a language system that differs from both L1 and L2. It is an approximation, a stage on the way to a second language. Learners begin with their L1, go through IL, and may or may not reach complete proficiency in L2. There is indeed a debate whether reaching native-speaker-like proficiency is possible or even desirable in adults. Interlanguage can be seen through the medium of errors that learners make, and people learning a given language all tend to make the same errors, regardless of their L1 background. Errors are different from mistakes. Mistakes are slips of the tongue; learners know the rule but don't apply it at the time of speaking. Errors are predictable and follow certain patterns. That is, as paradoxical as it sounds, they are rule governed. If someone says, "No go," he or she is likely in the first stage of acquiring negation and no amount of correction alone is likely to lead to, "I do not want to go." Depending on which theory you subscribe to, that learner will need more time, more practice, or more input to leave that stage and go on to another.

Because learners go through stages, acquiring certain items of syntax in relatively predictable fashion, some scholars (Krashen and Terrell 1996) have claimed that first and second language acquisition use similar cognitive/linguistic processes. The recipe for instruction that they offer amounts to treating the learner as a child learning the first language. That is, offer lots of input, just as children overhear language they do not fully understand. Keep the atmosphere of the classroom nonthreatening and allow for a sense of play. Let language wash over the learner.

Other scholars (Long 1996; Gass and Varonis 1989) focus on the role of interaction in the classroom. They say that learners need to work together on tasks that require the target language; these tasks should be meaningful and interesting. Still others (e.g., Swain 1985) say that the most important thing is to give learners a chance to look over the output they have produced, to in effect allow them to self-edit after an activity. In this way, they will see the distance between their own production and what the target language demands.

One aspect of learning a second language that is clearly different from learning a first is the presence of failure. Unless circumstances are very drastic, or unless there are physical or mental problems involved, everyone succeeds at L1 acquisition yet many do not succeed at L2. **Fossilization** is common; people get "stuck" at a certain level, frequently at the high-beginner/lower-intermediate level. Perhaps the greatest difference is the role of affective factors such as motivation and personality. People are generally motivated to learn L1 by wanting cookies, needing to go to the bathroom, wanting to be carried, and the like. People often learn a second language so they can pass a test or fulfill a requirement; this is not quite the same thing. People who are motivated may use tools such as strategies to improve their learning. They may use cognates as a way of expanding vocabulary; they may make flash cards; they may seek out opportunities to speak with others who know the language better than they do.

Language Ability

What do we mean when we say we know a language? In second language learning research, there have been a number of models of communicative language ability. We will present one model outlined in Bachman and Palmer (1996). This model is based on Bachman's 1990 model and is indebted to Canale and Swain (1980) and Canale (1983).

- *Language ability*, for Bachman, consists of *language knowledge* and *strategic competence*.
- Language knowledge may be further divided into *organizational knowledge* and *pragmatic knowledge*.
- Organizational knowledge is divided into *grammatical knowledge* (knowledge of vocabulary, morphology, syntax, and phonology/graphology) and *textual knowledge* (knowledge of cohesion and rhetorical organization; that is, how

- discourse is organized and the rules for holding texts and conversations together).
- Pragmatic knowledge consists of two main areas of knowledge: *functional knowledge* and *sociolinguistic knowledge*.
- Functional knowledge may be subdivided into knowledge of several types of speech acts: *ideational* (descriptions and classifications that help us express our place in the world); *manipulative* (those that affect other people, such as greetings, requests, and insults); *heuristic* (language used for teaching and learning); and *imaginative* (language for humor and poetry).
- Sociolinguistic knowledge is knowledge of dialects, registers, idiomatic speech, and cultural references.

All the above is subsumed under language knowledge. The other component in language ability is strategic competence. In earlier theories of communicative competence, such as Canale (1983), strategic competence was seen as a measurement of the ability of a speaker to rectify misunderstandings or to cope in situations when language ability failed, such as when the necessary word was missing from the speaker's vocabulary. Bachman sees strategic competence as a function of metacognition. It includes goal setting, assessment, and planning: the ability of the speaker to think through linguistic goals and how they will be realized. In a test situation, goal setting might involve choosing which tasks to do first or whether to do all the tasks at all. Assessment involves deciding if you have the resources to complete the tasks, and, if you do complete them, deciding how you did. Planning is perhaps self-evident: it involves making a plan to use your resources.

Pragmatics across Cultures

In Chapter 4, we discussed a subfield of linguistics called pragmatics. You'll recall that the study of pragmatics deals with the way we use language in context. For instance, when we call a friend's home, and ask "Is Emily there?" the person answering the phone understands that this is a request to speak with Emily. It would be odd (though children sometimes do this until they understand the true meaning) if the person on the other end answered "yes," the caller then said, "thank you," and then both parties hung up the phone. Situations requiring pragmatic competence occur frequently in our everyday conversations, and we are often completely unaware of them, making them one of the most difficult aspects of a second language to acquire. It is our lack of awareness of how pragmatic features operate even in our own language that can lead to miscommunication. These features become second nature to us. It is for this reason that the study of pragmatics across cultures is crucial to understanding various cultures and the way individuals (mis)communicate.

One of the most commonly studied areas within pragmatics is speech acts. In this section, we will discuss a few of the most oft-cited speech act studies and how these speech acts differ from culture to culture. It is clear that we need to learn more about this aspect of language along with pronunciation, vocabulary, word order, etc. When breakdowns occur within the realm of pragmatics, for example, we often attribute them to personality (individual or cultural) causes. This can be particularly disruptive as judgments concerning whether or not we want to have further interactions with individuals are often based on pragmatic misunderstandings. These misunderstandings are often the root of stereotypes assigned to various cultures as well (e.g., the French are rude, the Japanese are indirect, Americans are insincere). As a means of contrast, shortcomings with pronunciation, for example, seem to be easier for the listener to deal with, thus the listener is more capable of overlooking these shortcomings. Issues with pronunciation are rarely a part of whether or not we choose to remain friends with another person. Cohen and Olshtain (1993) provide an excellent example of pragmatic miscommunication (between a NS of English and a NS of Hebrew) that quite possibly wound up as a severed relationship:

Situation:	You promised to return a textbook to your classmate within a day or two, after Xeroxing a chapter. You held onto it for almost two weeks.
Classmate 1:	I'm really upset about the book because I needed it to prepare for last week's class.
Classmate 2:	I have nothing to say.

This interaction would appear incredibly rude to a NS of English as there is no willingness to apologize. However, when Cohen and Olshtain looked closer, they realized that the response was a translation equivalent to *I have no excuses*. If the

NS of English would have been aware of this, the miscommunication (and hard feelings) might have been avoided. As is clearly shown here, learners are not aware of the negative perceptions that go along with pragmatic errors. Instead, we attribute the pragmatic errors to a defect in a person—or an entire culture, as noted previously. This is especially true in situations where the learner is at an advanced level. If the learner's other linguistic features are all in place (e.g., pronunciation, lexicon), then it makes it that much harder to believe that the learner is still deficient is any other area (in this case pragmatic skills), which makes it even that much easier for the listener to assign issues of nonnativeness to personality attributes instead of shortcomings with the L2.

Acquisition of Pragmatics across Cultures

Pragmatic studies across cultures focus primarily on the acquisition and use of second language pragmatic knowledge. Most of the work in this area has centered on the analysis of speech acts. While multiple speech acts have now been explored (compliments, gratitude, complaints, greetings), we have chosen to discuss two of the most widely researched speech acts here, refusals and apologies.

What we know about refusals (and apologies for that matter) is that they do occur in most languages. However, refusals are not performed in the same way in each culture, nor do individuals feel comfortable refusing in the same situations around the world. Refusals affect second language learning because they are complex and require lengthy negotiation on the part of all speakers/hearers involved. Refusals also involve face-saving issues, as we are typically trying to minimize our noncompliance. Beebe, Takahashi, and Uliss-Weltz (1990) found that refusals fall into four main semantic formulas. Let's take someone's refusal of an offer to come over for dinner as an example:

1. Expressions of regret ("Oh, sorry.")
2. Excuses ("I have to work on my research paper.")
3. Offer of alternatives ("Maybe I could come by this weekend.")
4. Promises ("I'll have it done by then.")

You can see that a response could make use of all four: "Oh, sorry, I'll have to work on my research paper. Maybe I could come by this weekend. I'll promise to have it done by then." What Beebe, Takahashi, and Uliss-Weltz found was that these four formulas were used in all languages but that they differed in the order in which they were used. They found that NSs of Japanese (as well as NSs of Japanese learning English) began their refusals with positive opinions/empathy ("oh, that sounds like fun") and then followed with the excuse. Native speakers of American English, on the other hand, were found to use positive opinions, regrets, excuses, and then a statement similar to "I can't." The NS of American English is required to utilize more semantic formulas in a refusal than the Japanese speaker. The Japanese learner of English apparently transfers knowledge from the L1, which may in turn cause miscommunication between the Japanese and Americans. For example, while the Japanese feel that they don't need to hear anymore (enough is enough!) from someone offering a refusal, the American is typically expecting a more lengthy refusal from the Japanese. Both situations can cause hard feelings and misunderstandings.

Holmes (1989) has provided us with one of the most comprehensive studies of apologies from her New Zealand corpus of 183 naturally occurring exchanges. She found that women used apologies more often than men overall, that women apologized more to other women (and not as often to men), and that men apologized more to women than other men. Holmes's study also showed that women alluded more to the person being offended, while men's apologies alluded more to the offender. Studies such as this one shed light on how native speakers of a given language use speech acts in day-to-day conversations. This type of knowledge, when shared with learners of a language, can potentially be very useful. For example, if an NNS male uses multiple apologies in the workplace, he may be seen as more female in his tendencies and therefore looked upon differently based solely on these aspects of his speech.

When considering the use of pragmatics in second language learning, we need to deal with all of the social variables discussed in Chapter 4: relationship, status, age, sex, and who the overhearers are. Wolfson (1988) introduced the **Bulge Theory**, and many of these variables have been considered within the bulge. In basic terms, the bulge states that we find more similarities in the way we communicate between strangers (maximum distance, on one side of the bulge) and intimates (minimum distance, on the other side of the bulge). The center of the bulge is made up of nonintimates, status-equals, and acquaintances. Think for a moment of situations in which one might complain: we complain frequently with intimates (spouses, close friends) and with complete strangers (think of all the complaining we do in those long lines at Disney or at the bus stop when it's blazing hot). We have little to lose in these types of relationships: our spouses and close friends will always love us and forgive us, and we assume that we will never see strangers again. It is rare that we complain with nonintimates (e.g., coworkers) as this is the group that is the most risky to us in terms of saying the wrong thing—and more crucially, in the wrong way— and jeopardizing relationships and jobs.

The Acquisition of Pragmatic Features

Can language learners acquire pragmatic appropriateness as a result of interaction alone? Bardovi-Harlig and Hartford (1993) recorded ten NNSs of English over the period of one semester during two advising sessions. Their study of suggestions and rejections showed that the NNSs did indeed behave more similarly to their NS counterparts as the semester progressed. For example, learners used more suggestions and fewer rejections when interacting with their advisors. That is, students began to control their own course schedules by using more suggestions during interactions with their advisors rather than blatant rejections to their advisors' suggestions. As a result, the students were, overall, much more successful at the art of negotiating with their advisors. The NNSs used the appropriate speech act in most cases (i.e., they had learned when to make suggestions and when to make rejections); however, the appropriate linguistic form was not always used. For example, "Can I waive for this?" (Bardovi-Harlig and Hartford 1993) was used in an attempt to ask the advisor if she could get a waiver for a course her advisor felt she needed to take. One of the key insights to this study was that the learners continued to use fewer mitigators ("I was thinking . . . ") than NSs used in similar situations. Bardovi-Harlig and Hartford claimed that the nature of input may have played a key role here. The NNSs received consistent feedback regarding the choice of speech acts, but they did not receive feedback regarding the form of the speech act that they used.

The Teaching of Speech Acts and Speech Behaviors

Researchers have also been interested in whether direct teaching of speech acts to language learners is possible. A small guidebook written in Spanish for the sole purpose of making fun of the United States (and Americans) called *Guía del Típico Norte Americano* (Faul 1999) tells us in the opening paragraph that Americans are attracted to jokes of all kinds and that they use jokes and stupid comments instead of irony and wit. The author then says that Americans are unable to understand the latter two. This interpretation resonates with the findings from Nelms (2002) in which ESL learners were not only unable to interpret (or use) sarcasm in the target language (not in the classroom, but in daily face-to-face interactions), but also made self-determinations that Americans do not use sarcasm. First languages included Brazilian Portuguese, Arabic, French, Ewe (spoken in Ghana), and Spanish. All of the students were enrolled in intermediate-level courses at an English Language Institute. Data revealed that sarcasm is not a speech behavior that learners recognize at this level of proficiency in a second language.

In a debriefing session with the four learners in the Nelms study, three of them commented that sarcasm was a speech behavior "not used in American English." The Moroccan learner claimed that "Americans use little sarcasm . . . they show more respect towards one another." His session ended with an invitation for the researcher to "go to Morocco if you really want to get some serious exposure to sarcasm." The only sarcastic instances that the Spanish-speaking individual could recall were from his Spanish-speaking peers at the language institute.

It appears that sarcasm, like humor, shows up late in the acquisition process. This could be due to many factors. One such factor is that lower-level students have more novel features to attend to and are unable to recognize the often subtle features associated with sarcasm (e.g., facial features, gestures, or slight changes in intonation). Another factor may include the inherent differences in how sarcasm (and other speech acts/behaviors, for that matter) is realized across various languages. It is plausible that languages that realize sarcasm similarly to the target language may find an accelerated learning rate concerning this speech behavior. This was found to be true in Ard and Homburg (1992), who studied transfer as a facilitation of learning with learners of English whose first languages were Spanish and Arabic. They determined that Spanish speakers could focus more of their learning time on other aspects of the language (e.g., new vocabulary items) because such a large number of cognates exist between the native and target languages. We believe the same would hold true for those individuals whose languages realize sarcasm similarly, as these learners would be able to devote time to awareness of the important extralinguistic features involved in the interpretation of sarcasm. Having said this, it is also crucial to point out that obtaining empirical evidence would allow us to ascertain whether or not the exact opposite could also hold true. That is to say that much SLA research (e.g., Gass and Selinker 2001) highlights the notion that similarities between the L1 and L2 often go unrecognized, possibly leaving learners to believe that "only my language has sarcasm," for example.

The idea of whether or not pragmatic-related features can be learned in the classroom—and whether or not time should be spent on instruction—is highly controversial. While some (e.g., Cohen 1996) claim that most speech acts are highly routinized, thus allowing for predictability and presumably relative ease of instruction, others claim that there are far too many variations in the way we use speech acts. The latter see the teaching of speech acts in the classroom as a lower priority and most likely do not include it in any course curriculum. Think about the simple English greeting. Textbooks teach students how to say "Hi" and "Hello." How do students respond, then, when they come to the United States and someone says "hey" to them for the first time? Or instead of asking them "How are you?" someone asks, "What's up?" It would be next to impossible to teach the multiple variations of each speech act, including its form and function, in the limited time we have with most of our students.

However, many have shown that the teaching of speech acts (or related pragmatic features) can be highly successful. Olshtain and Cohen (1990) taught apology strategies (as well as the use of intensification as in "I'm deeply sorry" and emotionals as in "Oh my!") to a group of Israeli students learning English. The students were provided with three 20-minute lessons. After looking at students' posttests, the investigators determined that these fine points related to speech acts can indeed be learned in the classroom.

Similarly, Bouton (1988, 1990, 1992) showed that the teaching of implicatures (implied meanings) in the classroom was indeed successful. Implicatures are found frequently in daily conversations. The following exchange between a husband and wife illustrates this idea:

Wife: Did you like the meatloaf?
Husband: I'd rather have tacos next time.

The indirectly communicated idea, or implicature, is that the husband did not like the meatloaf and would prefer another meal in the future. He did not directly say this to his wife so she was forced to interpret the implied meaning of his utterance. Bouton's group of 30 nonnative speakers of English were able to successfully interpret implicature in English after a $4\frac{1}{2}$-year period. What Bouton tried to answer in his 1994 study was whether or not the students would have succeeded at dealing with implicatures with simple exposure to the language (after $4\frac{1}{2}$ years of living in the culture) or if instruction did in fact help them acquire this skill faster. He determined that the skills needed to interpret implicatures developed slowly and that particular trouble was found with two aspects of implicature: formulaic implicatures ("Is the Pope Catholic?") and implicatures that required specific cultural knowledge. He found that formal instruction, as could be predicted, was especially beneficial when dealing with the formulaic implicatures. At the end of one of his six-week pilot studies, the students receiving formal instruction performed just as well as those students who had been in the U.S. between 17 months and $4\frac{1}{2}$ years and who had not received any systematic training with regard to implicature. The more cultural and idiosyncratic types of implicatures, however, proved to be resistant to any form of instruction; the only successful tools in these situations were a significant amount of time spent in the culture and exposure to the target language.

In addition, Rose (1994) saw significant increases in his students' usage of pragmatic features when he used what he called "pragmatic consciousness raising." This amounts to explicit teaching of different speech acts and speech events through such means as teacher lectures and group brainstorming activities, which bring about similarities and differences interculturally with different speech acts such as apologies and thanking.

Teaching Scenarios

1. A textbook for intermediate ESL students tries to teach ways to apologize. It gives a list of about five formulas and then some practice. In light of what you know from this chapter and preceding ones, how effective is this likely to be? What needs to be considered?

2. You are advising students on what courses to take the following semester. An NS of English tells you, "I was hoping to take the grammar course," and an NNS of English (an international student) tells you, "I WILL take the grammar course." How do you respond to these two similar yet different situations? Do these responses have to do with the students' personalities, or is something else involved? If the NNS response would upset you, explain why.

Check Your Knowledge

1. Define interlanguage.
2. Give examples of how language learners transfer features of their first language into the language they are learning.
3. What are the differences between children learning their first language and adults learning a second language? What are the similarities?
4. What is the difference between a mistake and an error? Give some examples.
5. What is strategic competence?
6. How can stereotypes develop based on pragmatic miscommunication?
7. What are the arguments on both sides of the debate over teaching pragmatics in the classroom?
8. What might make it difficult for lower-level learners to interpret and use sarcasm?

Apply Your Knowledge

1. Think of an utterance that requires your hearer to give you a refusal (or any similar speech act). Use this same utterance, in a natural way, with at least five different individuals whose first language differs from yours. Do the same with at least two NSs of your language. Record each refusal (along with all relevant sociolinguistic variables) in a notebook and analyze them in terms of similarities/differences with your native language. Compare and discuss your findings in class.

2. Look at the following responses made by NSs and NNSs of English after having missed a very important job interview (errors have been omitted). Determine which were made by NSs and which were made by NNSs. What led you to your choice? How do you think each of the responses affected the hearer?

    I hope that you will consider me once again for an interview with your company.

    It is a must that you reschedule my interview time.

    I want to hear your reply to my request for another interview soon.

    I am still very much interested in your company.

    Last week I missed my interview time by mistake.

    I would be indebted to you if you would give me another opportunity.

    Please, please, please give me another opportunity.

    (Adapted from Maier 1992)

3. Think of as many misunderstandings involving pragmatic issues that you can. Do you think you will be able to avoid these misunderstandings in the future? Or do you think they will continue to be a source of friction?

4. Watch a rerun of *Seinfeld*, looking for one particular speech act. Design a classroom activity for learners of English using clips from the episode. If English is not your first language, do the same with any sitcom in your own language.

5. Watch a movie or TV show, pretending to be an NNS of the language the actors are using. What difficulties, in terms of pragmatics, might you experience?

Reflect

How real do you think the findings are from the various speech act studies in this chapter? Think back to your campus or your workplace about the number of apologies that men and women give (and to whom they are given) for example. Do you think they concur with Holmes's findings? Think back to the other speech acts that were discussed in this chapter as well. If you have the means, be a (polite!) eavesdropper on your campus or at your workplace and do an informal investigation of these speech acts for yourself.

Expand Your Knowledge

1. If you haven't yet, watch the video *The Human Language Series Part 2, Acquiring the Human Language: Playing the Language Game* (Ways of Knowing, Inc.). What similarities and differences between learning a first language and learning a second language did they present? Do you agree or disagree with the points that they tried to make? Think of examples from your own life to support/refute your opinions.

2. Read Spradley's (1979) work on conducting ethnographic interviews. Conduct an interview with someone who speaks a different L1 than you do and tape-record the interview. Find instances in which the interviewee uses various speech acts in ways that differ from native speakers of your own language.

3. Read Erickson and Schultz (1982). What is meant by the title *The Counselor as Gatekeeper?* Try to relate these experiences to your life or to the life of someone you know well.

4. Find out more about a particular speech act that interests you. For example, does it have predictable semantic formulas? How is it realized across cultures? How would you teach this speech act to students in an ESL classroom? Write a short report on your findings.

Suggested Readings

Alicia Martínez Flor, Ester Usó Juan, and Ana Fernandez Guerra, eds. *Pragmatic Competence and Foreign Language Teaching*. Castelló: Universitat Jaume, 2003.

Patsy M. Lightbown and Nina Spada. *How Languages Are Learned*. 2d ed. Oxford: Oxford University Press, 1999.

Kenneth R. Rose and Gabriele Kasper, eds. *Pragmatics in Language Teaching*. New York: Cambridge University Press, 2002.

Nessa Wolfson. *Perspectives: Sociolinguistics and TESOL*. New York: Newbury House, 1989.

Language Contact between Individuals and Cultures

1. Think about your contacts with other cultures and languages. What have you gained from those contacts? What frustrations have you experienced dealing with a culture or language not your own?

2. How would you describe this country's (or your state's) attitudes toward languages and language education? Is there a national policy, official or unofficial, toward English and other languages?

3. ⊞ What do you know about your ancestors' languages? What is the attitude in your home about language learning and keeping the language(s) of your ancestors?

Chapter 7 will help you understand issues of language and culture contact. It begins by describing contact between individuals, which sometimes necessitates code switching or foreigner talk. It continues by looking at contact that leads to the formation of pidgins and creoles. We next take up the common phenomenon of word borrowing and then address culture contact and change, including the individual response of culture shock. The chapter is next concerned with multilingualism and language policy, including language planning, diglossia, and societal bilingualism. Finally, we introduce the concepts of language maintenance, shift, death, and revitalization.

Individual Contact

At some level, all language and culture contact is individual. People talk to other people, even when they are speaking for their country. There are three important ideas that help us understand the ways people speak to others. The first, *code switching*, and the second, *accommodation*, help us understand ways that people affirm their membership in a culture. The third, *foreigner talk*, helps us understand how people interact with those who speak another language.

Code switching is the use of two or more languages or dialects within a single conversation. Code switching implies at least a minimal amount of bilingualism. Each interlocutor in a conversation has to assess how much language the other knows. It is a device used by bilingual speakers to convey certain attitudes toward the situation they find themselves in. Here's an example from a bilingual Spanish-English speaker. *Si tu eres Puertorriqueño* (if you're Puerto Rican), your father's a Puerto Rican, you should at least DE VEZ EN CUANDO (sometimes), you know, HABLAR ESPAÑOL (speak Spanish) (Poplock 1979/80). Blom and Gumperz (1972) reported on a conversation in Norway among university students home for the holidays. The conversation was an intellectual one, and the students, as they tried to dazzle each other with their brilliance, switched, unconsciously as it turned out, from the local Norwegian dialect used among friends to the more formal standard variety of Norwegian. When informed of their code switching, the students were somewhat embarrassed to have tried to one-up their friends in such a manner. Denison (1972) told of an argument in a tavern between husband and wife that happened in an area of northern Italy where people spoke standard Italian and dialects of Friulian and German. German was used in the home and Friulian in public in relaxed situations. While the man was talking with friends in Friulian, his wife entered and spoke to him in German, the language of the home. He answered in Friulian, the public language, but she resisted and continued in German. He capitulated and began to speak German. The unspoken argument, on top of the spoken, very real one, was whether their roles were at that time domestic or public. Different codes marked different arenas of discourse.

As we have seen, code switching may occur within sentences. This frequently happens in conversations among bilinguals. Sentences might begin in one language and end in another.

Code switching is often used in multilingual classrooms as an aid to student understanding or sometimes a way for the teacher to signal solidarity with students. An EFL teacher may speak the home language of the students while giving an English lesson, for example.

Communication Accommodation Theory (Giles and Powesland 1975) says that people adjust their language toward or away from their conversational partner. Their speech may converge, to become more like their partner's, or may diverge, to become less like their partner's. There are clearly reasons for convergence; it is most often the socially accepted thing to do. There are reasons for divergence, however. People do feel the need to differentiate themselves from others, and language is a clear way to do this. For instance, Welsh speakers may feel the need to assert their identity in conversations with monolingual English speakers and may choose to use a more pronounced Welsh accent than they normally use to do this.

Another model that concerns itself with linguistic identity is that of LePage,

(LePage et al. 1974) who maintains that children actively construct their linguistic identities. Language learning is a process of negotiating, through acts of identity, between family and society in order to align oneself with a particular group. Here, motivation plays a key role, but motivation is of course constrained by society itself. That is, a child may want to adapt a different identity through various linguistic markers but may be discouraged from doing so by parents (*"Don't get above your station"*) or society (*"Who do you think you are?"*)

Foreigner talk is a form of accommodation made "downward" to interlocutors who are believed to speak a language imperfectly. It is often used by members of a superordinate (more powerful) culture to members of a subordinate (less powerful) culture. Foreigner talk shares many features with child-directed speech. It is a simplified register: speech is slow, sentences are short, and syntax is simple. Vocabulary is concrete and at a generalized level (*car* and not *sedan*). Foreigner talk is also regularized: full forms, and not contractions, are used; false starts are kept to a minimum; and the topic of the sentence is often moved to the front to make it more salient *(you go—where?)*. Foreigner talk is also extended compared to more regular conversation: people try to repeat and use lots of synonyms and paraphrases. Stress and pauses may be exaggerated. Foreigner talk discourse is also simpler: conversation tends to be about the here and now, and there are a lot of choice questions (*X or Y?*). Indeed, there are many quick questions and answers in foreigner talk discourse, and topics do not get developed very fully. People feel free to drop the topic if comprehension is not demonstrated, instead of trying to repair misunderstandings.

Pidgins and Creoles

Pidgins are languages that come about as a result of contact between speakers of different languages who do not understand each other. They are, however, not individual responses to the problem of lack of communication; they are societal responses. Pidgins commonly arise in areas of trade, for example, along coastlines throughout the world. They may also arise as a response to people being gathered together, voluntarily or involuntarily. There has been a long-running controversy among linguists as to whether the Atlantic slave trade and subsequent plantation slavery system led to a pidgin that gradually developed into what is called African-American Vernacular English (AAVE), a dialect spoken by some, but not all, African Americans and by some who are not African American who identify with and value the dialect. That some sort of shared **Language of Wider Communication (LWC)** or **lingua franca** developed on the plantations or perhaps even before, in Africa, is less controversial than the claim that the AAVE of today still has ties to that LWC. Another example of plantation pidgin is the one developed in Hawaii to allow speakers of Philippine languages, Japanese, Chinese, Portuguese, and English to communicate with each other. Pidgins can be any combination of languages. Chinese Pidgin English was a combination of Chinese and English used in trade along the China coast. Russenorsk was a trade pidgin that combined primarily Russian and Norwegian languages.

The study of pidgins and creoles is full of controversy, perhaps because it is a relatively young field. There is not always agreement on basic terminology. It is generally accepted, however, that one language tends to supply most of the vocabulary for the pidgin; this is termed the *lexifier language*. Some would say this lexifier or superstrate language is chosen because it is the dominant or more powerful socially of the two languages; others put less emphasis on this point. In one view, the syntax of the pidgin is supplied by the substrate, less powerful, language; in another view, the emphasis is on the accommodation or negotiation that occurs in the construction of the syntax. (See Todd 1990 and Thomason 2001 for different overviews.)

What is clear is that, because the purpose of a pidgin is ease of communication about a relatively limited number of topics, the structure is kept simple. To show how difficult it is to make generalizations about the differences between pidgins and other languages, we can point out that pidgins are considered simplified partly because they have a limited number of vowels (5 to 7, versus 12 for English); Italian has 5 vowels and Arabic 3, however, and they are not considered simplified. The lack of inflectional morphemes (such as *–ed* and *–ing* in English) in pidgins has also been commented upon, but then English, compared to Spanish or other Romance languages, is very simple in its verbs. In fact, Tok Pisin (Papua New Guinea) has a more complex pronoun system than English, with two forms of *we*, one inclusive (you and I) and another exclusive (*I* and someone else not you). Clearly, power has some effect on the evaluation of languages. Pidgins and creoles have been stigmatized, sometimes even by the people who speak them, as *"barbarous"* or *"bastardized,"* at least partially because they have not been written down and thus were not seen as full languages. In many cases, there can be clear ethnocentric overtones in the evaluation of languages that sound something like European languages in many cases but are spoken by non-Europeans.

Pidgins are either useful or not useful. Restricted pidgins, such as those that grow up around military bases during times of war, die a quick death once the war is over. Extended or elaborated pidgins are used in a wide variety of circumstances across a relatively large multilingual area. Pidgins have no native speakers. Once the pidgin acquires native speakers, that is, once children are raised speaking it as their first language, it is termed a **creole,** which is a language formed of at least two others that serves a wide range of functions, as opposed to the pidgin's very narrow range.

Perhaps the most frequently encountered creole in the United States is Haitian Creole, the home language of many people in the South Florida, Boston, and New York metropolitan areas. The grammar of Haitian Creole shows influence from African languages, while the vocabulary has been strongly influenced by the French language. Traditionally, French and Creole have co-existed in Haiti, with French the formal language of newspapers, courts, and the schools and Creole the informal, everyday language. In the past 20 years, Creole has been permitted as a language of instruction in the first four grades of school, but there remains a stigma to the language. It is not considered the equal of standard French, even by those (90 percent of the population) who are monolingual speakers of Creole (Civan 1994). Here are two proverbs in Haitian Creole: Mwenbaw sal wap mande salon. (I give you a room and now you want my living room.) Byen pre pa lakay (Being close by doesn't mean you're home, or Being close to rich doesn't mean you're rich) (Civan 1994, p. 24).

When a creole exists in the same place as the lexifier language, there is often pressure on the creole to decreolize, to become more like the lexifier. For example, in Jamaica, there exists a Post-Creole Continuum, a range of varieties from a basilect through a mesolect to an acrolect. The **basilect** is the variety with the closest ties to Jamaican Creole. The **acrolect** is the standard English taught in schools. The **mesolect** lies between the two, along with a number of lects, so that the picture would be something like a rainbow. People control different parts of the continuum, as their lives dictate. As children go to school and on to university, they may choose to adopt the acrolect, at least in many situations, because of its role in access to jobs and status. Because language is a powerful resource and has a large role to play in people's identities, however, they may choose to recreolize, or shift their speech to the basilect, at least in some situations. British commentators have noted that in the United Kingdom, children and adolescents who speak Patois (a Caribbean Creole) have more creole features in their speech than their grandparents, many of them immigrants from the Caribbean in the 1950s, did.

Borrowing Language

Pidgins and creoles manifest a blending of two or more languages. There are also cases in which languages borrow from each other while staying relatively in tact. Perhaps the most obvious form of borrowing occurs in words. When a new thing or idea is introduced into a culture, the culture needs a name for it. When coffee was introduced into Europe, the Arabic word *kawatin* was borrowed and molded by the rules of the borrowing language into *coffee, café, Kaffee,* and so on. Japanese borrowed *koohii* from the European languages.

The borrowing language frequently changes the phonology of the borrowed word. Since Japanese does not allow syllables to end with a consonant (with the exception of *n*) *basketball* becomes *basuketobaru* and *steak* becomes *steiki*. Japanese loan words like *futon* and *karaoke* are Anglicized into pronunciations that Japanese speakers frequently cannot understand on first hearing.

A **calque** is a special kind of loan word in which component parts of the word are translated, thereby using the linguistic resources of the borrowing language. Thus, *skyscraper* becomes *Wolkenkratzer* (cloud scraper) in German, *gratte-ciel* (scrape-sky) in French, and *rasca cielos* (scrape clouds) in Spanish.

Words can be borrowed, and new words can be created from the resources of the borrowing language. Words can also be extended to label new concepts. Basso (1990) shows how Western Apache (southwestern United States) extended its entire vocabulary set for the body to the car. *Biwos* (shoulder) was used for *front fender, bigan* (hand and arm) for *tires, bizig* (liver) for battery, and so on. Basso explains that when cars and trucks were first introduced into Western Apache culture in the 1930s, they were thought to share with other items the ability to move themselves, so they were put into the *things that can move* category rather than the *things that must be moved by something else* category. From there, it was logical to extend the words used to name parts of people and animals to vehicles.

Linguists have argued that while words are frequently borrowed, the grammatical system is generally not. It seems that subordinators like *because* and conjoiners like *so that*, however, do get borrowed. Younger speakers of many languages in the countries formerly colonized by France in west Africa have adopted the French *mais* (but), *parce que* (because), and *pour que* (so that) into their speech. Affix borrowing is relatively rare, but it occurs; the suffix *-able/-ible*, originally borrowed into English in French loan words, spread to attain the status of a suffix that can be appended to any English verb to change it into an adjective (This margarine is *spreadable*. That plan seems *doable*).

Culture Contact and Change

Change can happen in a culture over time, as many small innovations add up to a larger result. This is sometimes described as cultural evolution. Culture can also change as a result of discovery or invention; the discovery of fire led to widespread culture change, as did the inventions of the Industrial Revolution. This sort of change is often called **innovation**.

Cultures may also change as a result of borrowing, or what anthropologists call **diffusion**. **Acculturation** is one kind of diffusion. Two cultures come in contact with each other. Depending on circumstances, there can be changes in one culture and not the other or changes in both cultures. The changes can be voluntary or involuntary, again depending on the circumstances.

When immigrants enter their new culture, they are faced with a choice regarding how much to assimilate, provided, that is, that they are allowed an opportunity to assimilate. **Assimilation** is the adoption of another culture by choice or necessity. Immigrants may choose to accommodate the new culture but not assimilate. In this strategy, immigrants do not fully accept the new culture but behave in ways that allow them to be successful in it. This often involves keeping an ethnic identity while still being involved in the larger culture.

Case studies in Gibson and Ogbu (1991) attest to the fact that keeping an ethnic identity backed by strong home support helps students succeed in school. Gibson (1991) calls this "additive acculturation." McNall and colleagues (1994) use the framework of Gibson and Ogbu in their study of Hmong immigrant high school students in St. Paul, Minnesota. They conclude that the Hmong students are successful because their situation combines a community emphasis on tradition and ethnic identity with parental support for education. That support is not uncondi-tional, however. Hmong parents in St. Paul have been vocal in criticizing aspects of the school culture that they see as contradictory to their own culture, such as moves the parents perceive as undermining their authority over their children.

Culture Shock

Culture shock is an individual response to changed circumstances. The term was introduced by Kalvero Oberg in the late 1950s to account for the reactions of people traveling or living abroad. The term has suffered some expansion over the years, so that a person moving from rural Maine to urban California may even be said to experience culture shock. We want to focus on the classic model of cultural shock as a U-shaped curve of five stages, using Pederson (1995) as a guide. Before outlining the stages, it is necessary to remind the reader that this is an individual process that different people will experience in different ways.

- The first stage of culture shock is often called the *honey-moon stage* because it is a time of excitement and optimism. The differences that are observed in the new culture are exciting and attractive.
- The *disintegration stage* is a time of frustration and helpless-ness. The new culture seems overwhelming, and the re-sponse of the newcomer is often depression or withdrawal.
- The third stage is the *reintegration stage*. The newcomer be-gins to fight back; anger may be directed away from the self and on to the new culture or its representatives, or the cul-ture may be rejected outright. The newcomer is defensive. The culture is the problem; the newcomer is not responsible.
- Gradually, the newcomer enters the fourth stage, the *au-tonomy stage*. The newcomer now has perspective on the culture. His or her opinions are balanced, objective, and may in fact be quite positive. Some people become self-styled "experts" in the culture. If the person has chosen to live in the new culture, he or she may experience some regression to the levels of disintegration or reintegration, then recover to re-experience the autonomy stage.

- Finally, certain people attain the fifth stage of *interdependence;* they acquire a new identity as a bicultural or multicultural person. Indeed, in some cases, people living outside their home culture may experience "reverse culture shock" when returning to it.

Multilingualism and Language Policy

We can distinguish individual bilingualism/multilingualism and societal bilingualism/multilingualism. Individuals may learn more than one language and often have to accommodate speakers of other languages. Multilingualism in societies is the norm for the world's population. Some countries have declared an official language. They may also officially recognize other languages as national languages. Often, the official language is the language of schooling, while national languages are used in government or otherwise as a means of uniting the nation. In the United States, annual attempts have been made in Congress to declare English the official language of the United States, so far to no effect. Several U.S. states do have official languages; Louisiana has made both English and French official languages, for example.

Status and Corpus Planning

The decision to make one or more languages official or national languages is part of a process known as **status planning.** Status planning involves the choice of a language for a given reason, and, by implication, the conferment of status on that language (and not on its competitor languages). An important reason Hawaiian was made a co-official language in Hawaii was to confer status on it as an attempt was being made to revive the language. Ethnic Hawaiians wanted their children to learn the language of their ancestors, and more resources would be available to them if the state recognized the language as official. For similar reasons, French was declared a co-official language with English in Louisiana in 1968. But which French was declared official? Presumably, the state legislature intended the French spoken in Louisiana to be valued. The French spoken in Louisiana is a variety descended from the language of the

Acadians, former residents of the Canadian Maritime Provinces. It is not the French of Paris, no better or lesser but different.

As this book is being written, East Timor (Asia/Pacific) is a new state after being ruled by Portugal for 400 years, by Indonesia for 24, and the United Nations for 2. The debate going on about which language(s) should be official encapsulates many of the issues of language planning. The new constitution has designated two official languages: Portuguese and Tetum, an Austronesian language. It has further designated English and Bahasa Indonesia as national languages. Portuguese was selected, though only about one-quarter of the population speaks it, because of its role in the independence movement; it is a symbol of resistance against Indonesia. Portuguese is also seen as vital to building a distinct East Timorese culture as well as a possible boost to the tourism industry, since it has close ties to French, Italian, and Spanish. Tetum was a court language in the 16th century and has been used since as a language of wider communication. It, too, is a symbol of resistance against Indonesia. It is also the liturgical language used by the local Roman Catholic Church. English and Bahasa Indonesia are useful as trade languages; Indonesia remains East Timor's major trading partner.

Corpus planning is the process by which decisions of standardization in a language are made official. Some countries, perhaps most famously France, maintain academies to rule on questions of neologisms (new words), grammar, spelling, and script. These academies are usually collections of distinguished writers who are asked to keep the language pure, free of foreign influence. The French Academy, for example, regularly criticizes the use of English loan words like *weekend* in French. In Israel and Ireland, committees invent new words as necessary; Hebrew and Irish Gaelic are both revitalized languages. That is, the languages almost disappeared (Hebrew was used as a religious language but not as a daily language of interaction). When they were revived in the 20th century, they did not contain words for some 19th and 20th century inventions, like the telephone, so the terms had to be made up by committee. South Korea, upon the recommendation of its National Academy of Korean Language, passed a law in 2000 to change its transliteration system, the system for converting Korean script into Latin letters (such as those on this page) to better reflect pronunciation. The letters K, T, P, and CH (as used together) were replaced by G, D, B, and J, respectively. Koreans were also asked to change the way they spell their (usually two) given names not as two words, as in the past, but as one word. Thus, the president at the time became not Kim Dae Jung but Gim Daejung. When the Soviet Union broke apart, many of its former countries were faced with the issue of whether to continue to write their languages, most of which had no family relationship to Russian, in the Cyrillic alphabet of Russian, in the Latin alphabet, or in some other script. Many chose the Latin script, at least partially in the case of the Turkic-speaking republics because it offered pan-nationalism, a bridge to Turkey (which had abandoned the Arabic script for the Latin one as part of its modernization campaign in the 1920s). (Landau and Kellner-Heinkele 2001).

Diglossia and Bilingualism

Ferguson (1959) defined **diglossia** as the use within society of two varieties of the same language for completely different functions. One variety, the high (H) language, is used in formal situations (such as church or political meetings) and usually in writing, while the other, the low (L) language, is used in informal contexts. This phenomenon is well known in Arabic-speaking countries, where classical Arabic is the H language and various dialects of colloquial Arabic serve as the L language.

Fishman (1980) extended the concept to two languages used in the same geographic area for different functions. For example, a subordinate language may be used in the home and the national or superordinate language used in the schools. Fishman has also distinguished cases in which individual bilingualism can exist with or without diglossia. Where there is bilingualism with diglossia, everyone in a community can use both languages, but the languages are used only in certain, functionally distinct ways. In Paraguay, almost everyone speaks Spanish and Guarani; Spanish is the formal language and Guarani is the informal language. In the case where there is bilingualism but no diglossia, most people are bilingual but use either language for any function. Fishman sees this situation as unstable and thinks that one or the other language may eventually decrease in use while the other increases in use.

In Fishman's model, there can logically also be diglossia without bilingualism, where one group in a given area will speak one language and another group a different language, as in a colonial situation. The last possibility is no bilingualism and no diglossia either, as in a monolingual country.

Language Maintenance and Shift: The Case of Immigrants

Many in the United States are familiar with the phenomenon of the loss of a heritage language within three generations. Indeed, the three-generation rule is the norm for immigrant societies. If your grandparents were immigrants (assuming they came from a non-English-speaking country and immigrated as adults), they likely were bilingual, with their original language being dominant (they would have had an accent and might not have had complete control over English grammar). Your parents were perhaps bilingual, or at least knew some phrases in their parents' original language. You might also know, or at least recognize, certain phrases (centered around food, customs, and perhaps oaths) but might not know much more than that of your heritage language. Different ethnic groups keep their languages longer, especially if they set up Saturday schools or after-school programs.

We can make predictions about *language maintenance*. In general, social, cultural, and economic isolation leads to language maintenance while social, cultural, and economic assimilation leads to language shift. Some specific factors that are implicated in language maintenance include number of speakers, length of residence in the country, proximity of the new country to the old, cohesive communities (voluntary or non-voluntary), economic mobility, and group identity. If the community is large and concentrated, it has a better chance of keeping its language. If the ethnic community has been long established, the chances are greater that it will be assimilated into the larger culture and lose its language. If the home country is far away, costs will usually keep people from visiting; the converse happens in the southwestern part of the United States, where there is frequent movement of people back and forth between Mexico and the United States, which keeps Spanish alive. More recent immigrant groups are often segregated from the larger community; this segregation is sometimes voluntary but may also be the result of discrimination in housing or lack of economic opportunities. If the community is homogenous, it will tend to keep its language, as people go about their daily lives in the home language. As their economic status improves, assuming improvement is fostered by the society, people often move out of the more cohesive communities and the communities break up and lose their language. For all that, if a language is important to a group's identity, it will be kept, at least for a while. Cultural and religious organizations often lead the way in language maintenance (Paulston 1994).

While we have focused on the immigrant experience, language maintenance and shift are issues in bilingual communities. Gal (1978) has shown how a stable bilingual situation in Austria changed over time as the respective reputations of the two languages changed. In this particular area of Austria, people were bilingual in Hungarian and German for hundreds of years. As industrialization and urbanization increased, however, German became the language of modernity and economic development, while Hungarian was identified with the peasant economy. As a result, the number of Hungarian speakers declined as people allied themselves with the new.

Language Death and Endangered Languages

Sometimes, language shift goes so far as to lead to language death. There are about 6,000 languages in the world. Ninety percent of the world's population speaks 100 of those languages. Perhaps one-quarter of the world's languages have fewer than 1,000 speakers. We can sometimes pinpoint the death of a language, as its last speaker dies. Steps are being taken in some cases to revitalize languages through education and in other cases to at least document the language before it disappears. This is done through compiling texts in the language and writing dictionaries and grammars. A number of non-governmental organizations are coordinating these efforts. As we lose languages, we are losing human diversity. Languages provide insights into cultures, and having fewer languages reduces the number of perspectives on life.

Smaller languages tend to get displaced by larger, more powerful ones. The most powerful language today is English. Its popularity has led some to call it a murderous language. As people give up their own languages for English, some of those languages become endangered. English is powerful for historical reasons (the history of imperialism in the 19th and 20th centuries), current economic/political reasons (American hegemony as the sole superpower), and media/cultural reasons (the spread of American popular culture throughout the world). Over 95 percent of the scientific articles written are in English, and it is an official or national language in some 60 countries.

Yet, though English is the global language, it exists as a number of Englishes. Kachru's (1992) model of circles has been very influential. His Inner Circle comprises nations where English is a dominant native language (the United States, the United Kingdom, Canada, New Zealand, Australia). The Outer Circle contains countries that have a long history of English being a second language (India, Pakistan, Kenya, Malaysia, Ghana, Panama, the Philippines, etc.). The Expanding Circle is where English is a widely studied foreign language (Japan, Korea, China—in effect, the rest of the world).

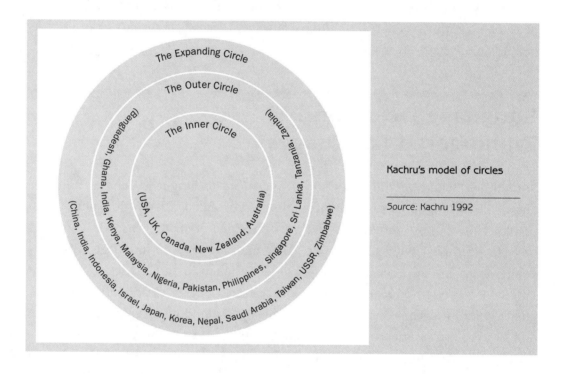

Kachru's model of circles

Source: Kachru 1992

Because there are so many Englishes, there has been debate on standards. Who does English belong to? What is correct? There are dictionaries of Australian, Canadian, New Zealand, and South African English, all of which have words not found in the others. Pronunciation obviously differs. From our point of view, the most interesting phenomenon is the relationship of language and culture. English is spoken in Indian culture in culturally pragmatically appropriate ways while it is spoken quite differently, but still appropriately, in Nigerian cultural ways. Is it all English? Yes.

Language Revitalization

Language revitalization is the process by which endangered languages are returned to reasonably common use. A frequently mentioned example of language revival is Maori, the indigenous language of New Zealand. Recent figures show only about 10 percent of the Maori speakers under the age of 45 use the language at some time during the day, while 56 percent say they never use the language at home (Benton and Benton 2001). This decline in the use of Maori has been going on for some time; children were routinely put into transitional bilingual education classes, with the goal of making them monolingual English speakers. In the early 1980s, a grassroots movement of parents began the *kōhango reo* (Language Nest) preschools, where Maori children from English-speaking homes would go to learn Maori through play, songs, games, and stories. While by no means universal now, the preschools have increased the number of young Maori speakers. There are also now a small number of Maori-medium primary schools in which Maori children learn English around the age of eight, after they have become literate in Maori first. Family use of Maori has been encouraged by the Ataarangi Movement, which teaches the language in groups at home. Despite the widely publicized success of the programs, Maori is still in danger of decline. Other groups have used the Maori *kōhango reo* model to try to revive indigenous languages. One example is the Navajo nation, which has used the system in its Head Start schools (Lee and McLaughlin 2001).

Teaching Scenarios

1. A junior high school teacher has a number of students from China in his class. In conversations outside of class, they tend to code-switch between Chinese and English, often within the same sentence. The teacher feels that this is harmful to the students' English development. Why might the students be code-switching? What would you tell the teacher?

2. Some members of the school staff speak rather loudly to students from other countries. However, they make no effort to slow down their speech or eliminate idioms or slang. Is this wise? What would you tell the staff if you could?

3. Your school has an "English only" policy for speech. It also has a large number of immigrants. What are the possible group (not individual) consequences of this policy? Is the policy a good idea? Does the language(s) the immigrants speak factor into your answer?

☑ Check Your Knowledge

1. What do Communication Accommodation Theory and acts of identity have to do with constructing a linguistic identity?
2. What are the characteristics of foreigner talk?
3. How are pidgins and creoles formed?
4. How do cultures change?
5. What is culture shock? What are its stages?
6. What are status planning and corpus planning?
7. What is meant by language maintenance and language shift?
8. What is meant by language death?

9. Be able to define these terms:

code switching

code mixing

Language of Wider Communication/lingua franca

basilect/mesolect/acrolect

calque

assimilation

innovation

diffusion

acculturation

diglossia

Apply Your Knowledge

1. Try speaking the foreign language you speak best with someone who speaks it as a native language. What accommodations did you notice that person making?

2. Volunteer at a center that teaches English to speakers of other languages. What aspects of foreigner talk did you find useful in communication?

3. Interview a student from another country or someone who has recently returned from study abroad about his or her experience with culture shock. For example, when were signs of culture shock first evident? What were these signs?

Reflect

How has language(s) shaped your identity?

Expand Your Knowledge

1. 🎬 Watch *Daughters of the Dust*, a film about the South Carolina/Georgia Sea Islands, and write a report about it. What features of pidgins and creoles did you notice in the speech of the characters?

2. Research recent attempts to make English the official language of the United States. What are the arguments (both pro and con)?

3. Research recent attempts to outlaw bilingual education. What are the arguments (both pro and con)?

4. Find out more about pidgins and creoles. Research one in some depth and report to the class.

5. Research the findings linking African-American English historically to creoles. What is the current state of research on this question?

6. Find out about the language policy of a country you are interested in.

7. 🎬 View *Mississippi Masala*. What problems were there in the relationship between Meena and Demetrius from the communities' point of view and the family's point of view?

Suggested Readings

Colin Baker and Sylvia Prys Jones, eds. *Encyclopedia of Bilingualism and Bilingual Education*. Clevedon, UK: Multilingual Matters, 1998.

Sandra R. Schecter and Robert Bayley. *Language as Cultural Practice: Mexicanos en el Norte*. Mahwah, NJ: Lawrence Erlbaum Associates, 2002.

John Edwards. *Multilingualism*. New York: Routledge, 1994.

Varieties of Language

1. What is Standard English? Did you go to school for the first time speaking Standard English? What parts, if any, of your dialect were nonstandard?

2. What social class are you? How do you know?

3. How did your friends at high school show that you were a group?

4. ▦ What are the differences between women's and men's speech?

Chapter 8 will help you understand the interactions between language, ethnicity, social class, age, and gender and how these interactions affect educational opportunity.

Ethnicity and Language

Everybody speaks a dialect. Dialects can be regional (based on geography) or social (based on societal status). Some dialects are valued, and others are stigmatized. The Appalachian U.S. dialect, for example, is often (and wrongly) stigmatized in that its speakers are assumed by speakers of other dialects to be uneducated "hillbillies" and quite likely racists. The United States does not have a history of any sort of official agency that watches over correct usage, so there are some differences in what people consider "standard American." Most people would probably identify the language of radio and TV to be standard, however.

One variety that is frequently (and wrongly) stigmatized is what linguists call African-American English or African-American Vernacular English (AAVE). This variety has variously been called *slang, street language, broken English,* and so forth, even by those who use it. It is none of those things; it is a dialect. There is no one-to-one match between the dialect and being African American. In fact, some European Americans, Asian Americans, and Latinos raised in African-American neighborhoods speak this dialect fluently. Many African Americans do not use it at all. Many people code switch between African-American English and Standard English. The percentage of use of African-American English tends to be higher in working-class communities than in middle-class communities.

Linguists have formally described the features of African-American English and argued about its history. These debates are too technical for us to address here, but we encourage those interested in linguistic description to consult our suggested readings. As we noted in Chapter 7, a central question in linguistics concerns itself with the amount of influence west African languages have had on African-American English. A prominent position is that African-American English is essentially a decreolized creole based on contact between west African languages and English during the slave trade.

At a 1973 conference, the psychologist Robert Williams coined the term *Ebonics*, combining ebony and phonics. *Ebonics* originally was to be used as a descriptive term for the common features of all the languages used by descendants of the African slave trade. Over time, it came to be used, quite contrary to original intentions, as a synonym for African-American English (Baugh 2000).

When in 1996 the Oakland, California School Board announced a plan to recognize Ebonics as the home language of most of the students in their majority African-American district, a great controversy broke out. The board felt that declining achievement among African-American students could be helped by essentially treating Ebonics speakers the same as bilingual students (i.e., as students whose home language was not the same as the school's language). While there are good reasons to begin with what students already know (Rickford 1999), the media made it seem as if Oakland was "teaching Ebonics" rather than Standard English. The U.S. Department of Education, fearing it would have to increase bilingual education funds to Oakland, almost immediately declared that Ebonics was not a language but a dialect of English. In fact, most linguists would agree that African-American English is one of many dialects of English. Nevertheless, linguists defended this dialect as being rule governed and acceptable as any other (Perry and Delpit 1998; Baugh 2000).

It is important to stress that simply acknowledging the rule-governed behavior of African-American English or even teaching Standard English alone will not improve educational opportunities. Schools exists in a context. In many communities, the real issue is not language but underfunded and understaffed schools. The explanation for substandard schools involves history and politics and is beyond our scope here.

Social Class and Language

Social class is notoriously hard to define. Most Americans call themselves "middle class." Even those in the upper 5 percent of incomes do so. Classical American sociological theory has seen class as a function of power, education, income, and type of work done. Find the relevant information, and you have the class. But what of highly educated teachers who cannot find full-time jobs and thus have low incomes? Is class something you are born into and never leave? If you don't work but live with someone who makes a large salary, what class does that make you?

Perhaps the greatest danger in attempting to measure socioeconomic status is in labeling children *at risk* because they fit into certain categories. Educational researchers have found a number of factors that correlate with success (or lack of it) at school. For example, in a longitudinal study following children from entering kindergarten to the first grade, researchers defined the following as *risk factors:* coming from a single-parent family or a family that receives welfare, having a mother who did not finish high school, and having a parent who speaks a language other than English at home (U.S. Department of Education 2003). This simply means that there was some association between these factors and lower-level performance in the first years of school. It does not mean that every child with these factors automatically did not succeed. Some children with these risk factors, in fact, excelled. Notice that all of these factors are potentially measures of income, though they certainly need not be. People who do not finish high school or who do not speak English well will not be considered eligible for certain jobs. On the other hand, plenty of middle-class parents choose to speak a language other than English in the home, often in order to raise their children to be bilinguals. The important point is that this labeling can have the effect of branding children as deficient before they arrive at school. We must take these labels with a grain of salt and remember that saying two things are correlated simply means there is a relationship. Correlations do not prove causality, do not prove that there is a cause and effect.

Basil Bernstein (1971) is both one of the most famous and the most criticized researchers of the relationship between language and social class. Bernstein was particularly interested in socialization and cultural reproduction, in who controls the ideas and symbols of society and how those symbols are maintained or changed. Following Marx, he said that the social structure of a society determines the behavior of its members. He focused on the influence social structure has on the way children are socialized.

Bernstein saw that those in power in a given society have control not only over the economy but over cultural capital, including language. (At a very basic level, this is seen in how the language of the poor is criticized as slang or as an ill-formed reflection of unclear thought.) Social class, for Bernstein, influences work, education, and the family. The class system puts people in certain categories and ranks them. By belonging to these categories, people are socialized in certain ways that are valued or stigmatized by the larger society.

Bernstein spent 30 years elaborating his theory. We will focus, as the standard textbooks and encyclopedias do, on the earliest, most basic versions of the theory. This is in some sense unfair, because Bernstein later contextualized and presented his thought somewhat differently (though he did not repute the early work). We do so because the early work was the most influential in general thinking about education. We also do so because we cannot begin to synthesize the five substantial volumes, each building on the other, in which Bernstein refined the theory.

In Bernstein's earliest theory, linguistic meaning can be *universalistic* (not tied to a given context) or *particularistic* (tied to a given context, local relationships, and local structures). In this view, working-class communities tend to be tied more closely to particular local conditions than is the middle class. Working-class communities share understandings, so speakers do not need to articulate meaning to each other. Meaning is implicit and understood. This setting leads to a **restricted code**, with limited and predictable grammatical and lexical choices. This is an inflexible form of language that is seen to make generalization and logical reasoning difficult. Authority in the working-class family exists within a context and is "positional." Hierarchies are important. The answer to "Why?" is "Because I said so" or "Because I'm your mommy." A restricted code conflicts with many of the expectations of school, so working-class children according to Bernstein tend not to do as well as middle-class children do in school.

According to Bernstein, middle-class children also have an **elaborated code** that is oriented toward universalistic meaning, one that is said to make complex reasoning and abstract thinking relatively easy. They tend to come from situations that are person oriented, where discussion and criticism is the norm, and where roles are flexible. Discipline is likely to be negotiated with hypotheticals ("If you're good, we'll go to McDonald's"). Partly as a result of controlling this elaborated code, middle-class children have less difficulty working their way through school.

To be fair to Bernstein, he was not saying that these differences are cognitive. He was saying that working-class children did not succeed in school *because* they did not have the proper language. The class system denied it to them. In fact, he stressed that everyone in the middle class has both restricted and elaborated codes at their disposal, that the middle class in fact does not speak abstractly all the time (that is, they code switch). He gives the example of a husband and wife who speak in a restricted code to each other about a movie (because they have both seen it) and then speak about the movie in an elaborated code to friends who have not seen the movie (and thus need lots of contextualization). The working class needed to add a code. Still, many saw Bernstein as blaming the victims, as making failure seem natural.

Labov (1969/1972), in his article "The Logic of Nonstandard English," criticized Bernstein's work as being part of the *verbal deprivation* characterization of working-class language. Labov looked at interviews with two African Americans, one working class and the other upper-middle class, and showed that in fact the working-class speaker gave pithy, interesting answers to the interviewer's questions, while the upper-middle-class speaker rambled and generally said very little in a lot of words. Much has been made of this contrast. While the results are interesting, we cannot, however, draw too many conclusions from the behavior of two people.

Codes were later considered by Bernstein to be aspects of discourse. Bernstein outlines two kinds of discourse, *vertical discourse*, which has its origins in official institutions and is coherent and explicit, and *horizontal discourse*, which has its roots in the everyday world and is context dependent (Bernstein 2000). In his later work, he discussed an earlier study of working-class and middle-class seven-year-olds who were asked to group pictures of common objects in any way they wished. They were then asked for the rationale for the grouping. Initially, the working-class children grouped the pictures according to personal experiences ("I eat these. I don't like these."), while the middle-class children grouped the pictures into more abstract categories such as *vegetables* and *things in the sea*. When asked to regroup and reanalyze the pictures, the working-class children stayed with their life-experience groupings, while the middle-class children added life-experience groupings to their academic groupings (i.e., the middle-class children changed their way of grouping whereas the working-class children did not). Thus, the middle-class children had two codes available to them but, in a "test situation," used the standard discourse of the school as their default answer.

The work of Milroy (1987) in Belfast is relevant here for two reasons. This research studied three communities that spoke a low-prestige variety of English. People in these communities were linked by high-density social networks, clusters based on kinship, occupation, and social status; people were members of the same extended family, worked the same type of job, and drank at the same pubs. The picture the research draws is of a tightly knit working-class community, giving some support to Bernstein's characterization. Perhaps more importantly, the Milroy study is taken to show how people construct their own identities by self-consciously using certain forms of language. People are not, in this view, essentially working class or middle class but rather behave, or perform, in class-identified ways.

How Students Experience Class

In some studies, preschool children have been able to accurately sort pictures of *rich* and *poor*. The ability to make finer distinctions, to recognize symbols of class (a silver tea set, for example) seems to increase throughout elementary school. Evaluations of the reasons for poverty change too. Researchers have seen a change from evaluating poor people as bad or lazy in the upper grades of elementary school to making fewer blanket statements and eventually even offering socioeconomic reasons for poverty in high school (Chafel 1996).

In a study comparing low-income and high-income adolescents, Brantlinger (1994) found that low-income students believed their teachers looked down on them, were "snobbish," and preferred affluent students. The higher-income students assumed teachers liked them. They evaluated teachers in terms of personality and classroom interaction, while lower-income students appreciated teachers who took an interest in them and did not try to humiliate them.

In a longer study (1993), Brantlinger found social class "ubiquitous" in schools. Affluent adolescents disapproved of their low-income peers, thinking them stupid, immoral, and scary. Low-income students felt rejected and humiliated by their peers, as well as by the school staff, who they felt were on the side of the high-income students. It seemed that the low-income students more often explained disciplinary decisions as being based on social class than did the higher-income students, who identified classroom achievement or good behavior as reasons they got in less trouble than their peers did.

Much in Brantlinger's work reinforces the findings of Eckert's 1989 study of *jocks* and *burnouts* in a Michigan high school. Many of the middle-class students in the school organized their lives around extracurricular activities. These middle-class, generally college preparatory, students are frequently called *preps* or *preppies* (from prep school) or *soshes* (from *socials*); at this school, they were called *jocks*. The other large group at the school did not expect to go on to college but rather expected to stay in the old neighborhood among their friends and get a blue-collar job. These students are often called *hoods*, *greasers*, and *stoners*, and, in this school, they were called *burnouts* or *jellybrains* as a result of their purported drug use. There were some in-between students, but many caught in the middle expressed discomfort. Jocks stereotyped burnouts as drug-taking troublemakers without ambition. Burnouts stereotyped jocks as overly ambitious and competitive as well as elitist. Women in both groups had special stereotypes; the jock women as "phony" and the burnout women as sexually promiscuous. Eckert found all this beginning sometime in junior high school. At the start of junior high, there was crossover in group membership; burnouts still participated in after-school activities such as football and cheerleading. By the end of junior high, lines had been drawn.

Eckert found the two groups differentiated themselves through linguistic markers, among other things. She found a correlation between group membership and the way certain vowels were pronounced. That is potentially interesting in itself, but it is also another example of how people consciously mold their behavior to show membership in a group, how identity can be a matter of personal choice rather than anything fixed.

Age and Language

Eckert's work is one of the most important linguistic studies we have of high school students. She shows how adolescents seek autonomy by joining groups and marking those groups off by language. To be sure, adolescents differentiate themselves from children and adults and from other adolescents by a variety of means, including clothing and group values. Here, of course, we will focus on language.

Even people who know little about language comment on the slang of young people. Writers of TV shows attempt to put the latest slang in their characters' mouths, ignoring, or perhaps not understanding the fact that as soon as a non-student knows the slang term, it is probably already outdated. That is because the purpose of slang is partially to reinforce group identity. People use slang to separate themselves from others. They also use it to have fun and to be innovative with language, and, particularly in the case of young people, to be a little rebellious. While saying what slang is, it's also important to reinforce what slang is not. Slang is not dialect. Dialects are regional and social, while slang is used by small groups as an in-group language.

Eble had collected a corpus of more than 10,000 slang terms before writing her 1996 book on college slang. She collected ten slang words from each student in her introductory linguistics classes at the University of North Carolina at Chapel Hill over a 20-year period. The nature of slang is to be ephemeral, but four words were shared in Eble's surveys of 1972, 1980, and 1987: *bad* (meaning *good*), *bummer* (an unpleasant experience), *wheels* (a car), and *slide* (an easy class) (Eble 1996). This list illustrates the fact that slang can also be regional or even local. While *bad, bummer,* and *wheels* are familiar to those of us who live outside North Carolina, and indeed have entered general use (in TV shows, for example), *slide* is not familiar.

Slang is not the only linguistic way adolescents mark themselves off. Within groups, they may speak very elliptically, leaving things out that members of the in-group understand. Certain words may have vivid connotations for the group. Another way adolescents set themselves apart is through language play. Labov (1969/1972) studied signifying among African-American adolescents in New York City. *Signifying,* also called sounding, woofing, or playing the dozens, is a speech act in which (usually) young men ritually insult each other's families or each other. Some of Labov's examples that can be printed here include: "Your mother wear high-heeled sneakers to church!" "Your mother so old she got spider webs under her arms." "Your mother raised you on ugly milk."

Labov shows how the dozens are different from personal insults. They are highly ritualized and have their own rules. They call for a certain kind of response, and someone who gets angry or responds in an inappropriate way loses the contest. Audience is also essential to playing; signifying tends not to be done one-on-one.

While Labov locates signifying within youth culture, Mitchell-Kernan (1972) shows how it is important in the larger African-American community as a method of indirection. For example, she shows how people can be gently admonished through being signified on.

Ritual insults are part of other cultures as well. Labov mentions some ritual insults used by European-American adolescents that are not as complex as those of their African-American counterparts (most of the European-American insults involved excrement). Turkish adolescents insult each other's mothers and sisters and accuse each other of homosexual acts in very stylized ways.

Another interesting aspect of age and language is the **high rise terminal (HRT)**. The HRT is a rising intonation on an utterance that is actually a statement; this is typically reserved for questions in English. This is prevalent with teenagers in the English-speaking world (especially in New Zealand, Australia, and the United States). For example, someone from this age group might say "I went to school and then I played baseball" with rising intonation at the end of the words "school" and "baseball." The question as to where this speech style originated is still unknown. Some think it began in New Zealand, was carried to Australia, and then came to the United States. The function of the HRT is also in question. Since the rising intonation is viewed as a question, the speaker often receives confirmation that he or she has been heard and understood. Because this is a relatively new phenomenon, it will be interesting to observe the speech patterns of today's teenagers to see if they carry this form with them into their adult lives. It therefore remains to be seen whether or not the HRT will become the norm in adult communities over time.

Gender and Language

How did you answer the question about the differences between women's and men's speech from the beginning of the chapter? If you asked ten people on the street if women and men spoke differently, a majority would probably say *yes*. People would probably say that women tend to use different words than men (*lovely, mauve*), use fewer taboo or swear words, perhaps use more emphasis in speech (*that's so pretty*), and so on.

Anthropologists have noted that some languages have phonological and morphological differences in women's and men's languages. That is, a word will be much the same, but one sound within that word, or perhaps a certain suffix, will be used by women and another by men. Sometimes entire words are different. For example, in Japanese, women and men use different pronouns in certain situations. The informal first person pronoun *(I)* for women is *watashi* or *atashi* and for men *boku* or *ore*. These differences do not amount to separate *languages*, however. (See Coates 1993 for a good overview of language and gender research.)

Robin Lakoff was an early researcher of gender differences in language. She accepted that there were differences in women's and men's speech but said that these differences were a result of a power differential in society: because men held more power, women spoke the language of the powerless. For example, women, she said, *hedge* their opinions with "sort of" and "a little" (Lakoff 1975). This gives the impression that women are not secure in their opinions, but that is not completely accurate. Women are in fact involving their conversation partners by using this device.

Other researchers, like Maltz and Borker (1982) and Tannen (1990), considered gender differences in speech as a product of two distinct cultures with different rules of speaking. This approach has been criticized as essentializing women and men, ignoring individuality to focus instead on categories (and static, unchanging categories at that). These critics argue that we should look at the *who, what, when, where, why,* and *how* of language use to try to find out how people use language in specific ways. In fact, gender differences in language are best seen not as *dichotomies* but as *preferences*. It should also be noted that speech differences between men and women are just that: *differences*. Neither style is inherently good or bad, and knowing how the two differ can serve to facilitate communication.

Much recent research on age and gender has adopted a *community of practice* model. Rather than looking at fixed categories like class and gender, researchers have looked at the activities people do together and how that activity and the language used construct identity.

Gender and Education

Many studies have shown that girls have more verbal ability than boys, as measured by test results, by learning to read faster, and by performance on writing assessments. This has been a cause for concern, insofar as other studies have indicated an advantage for boys in math and science. The concern is that girls will be placed into majors and jobs in the arts and humanities and boys in the (higher-paying, more prestigious) sciences. Programs to interest girls in careers as scientists and engineers have increased markedly in recent years. For reasons that are not entirely clear, more recent results are mixed, however, and the gap seems to be narrowing.

Studies in the 1970s and 1980s found that teachers spoke more to boys, including giving boys more praise and blame than they did girls. Teachers also asked boys a wider range of question types; girls were asked fewer open-ended questions that called for lengthy responses. Teachers gave boys the advantage of more wait time when answering questions, reprimanded girls—and not boys—for calling out answers without being called upon, and directed their gaze to boys more often than girls. Both men and women teachers acted in the same way. In the 1990s, there was less research of this nature, perhaps because there was less interest in gender differences in general. Some of this conventional wisdom is beginning in fact to be challenged, but there is no new picture to take the place of the old one thus far (Swan 1992; Sunderland 2000a).

As we have noted, many scholars have suggested that setting up gender-based oppositions is not helpful because doing so erases individuality and essentializes gender. Measured classroom differences are the results of averages, *all the girls, all the boys*. Sunderland (2000b) points out that in her study two boys received lots of attention from the teacher. If we looked only at the categories *boys* and *girls*, we might conclude that boys get more attention than girls. However, if these two boys are subtracted from the mix, the amount of attention paid to boys and girls in this classroom is basically equal.

In second language learning, issues of classroom interaction are also important. Many second and foreign language classrooms use a large amount of group and pair work, and the potential of men to dominate the activity in mixed-sex groups, particularly in cultures where male dominance is a given, has been a matter of concern. Also of concern has been the matter of adopting the gender roles assigned people in the language/culture being acquired. Can a learner transfer a familiar gender identity into a new language, or do the rules of that new language require a different identity in the learner? Because gender roles are cultural, a new culture may require gender to be performed differently. Women, for example, may be expected to acquire (and may resist acquiring) what has been labeled "women's speech." People may feel that prescribed ways of speaking the L2 make them feel more masculine or more feminine (in so far as those words make any sense) than they want to, and they may resist language learning (Pavlenko 2001).

Finally, the role of women in the acquisition of new languages by immigrants, in language maintenance and shift, has been the topic of much debate. There has been an ongoing debate in sociolinguistics about the role of women in language change in general, with no definite answers given. In fact, again, we must say that generalizing to entire genders may be inherently false. Some have said that women in general are a force against language change, that they are resistant to adopting new words and new structures. Others have claimed that women are often in the forefront of language change, being open to new words and structures. Much depends on how and where one does the research. In second language learning, this debate is narrowed to focus on the role women have in acquiring the new culture and language. In many groups, women are expected to stay home and mix with the larger community as little as possible. In these communities, women may be very important in maintaining the home language but may also have problems learning enough language to interact with school staff, for example. Other women may play a large role in facilitating language change for the whole family as a go-between between home and the larger culture. (See Pavlenko et al. 2001 for recent research on gender and second language learning.)

Teaching Scenarios

1. You work in a school district with a large percentage of African-American students. Some teachers refer to AAVE, the language of some of the students, as "slang." These teachers think that "slang" should be eliminated from the language that students use at school. What are the issues involved here?
2. Some of the teachers in your high school are worried that young female students are not confident in the opinions they express in class. Based on the findings of Chapter 8, what might have given them this impression?

☑ Check Your Knowledge

1. What was the Oakland Ebonics controversy about?
2. What are the differences between elaborate and restricted codes?
3. How did Labov's findings contradict Bernstein's findings?
4. How was social class important in high school according to Eckert's study?
5. What are the various explanations for why language differs between women and men?
6. Be able to define these terms:
   Ebonics
   elaborated code
   restricted code
   slang
   ritual insult
   HRT

Apply Your Knowledge

1. Here are excerpts from two speeches about the closing of a steel mill. What is the social class of each speaker? How do you know?
   a. "Kensington Steel never lost a dime in this town. Made money on us is what they did. Now they're pullin' out. No way!" The crowd went into a frenzy, and Damjani waved his arms for several minutes before he was able to be heard. "I'm taking up too much time. The man says it a lot better than I ever could; he says it so everybody knows, so everybody sees it like it really is. You know who I mean."
   b. "The final demolition of the plant . . . will be postponed by winter weather, at least until April. But remember, demolition is the reason for the closing in December.

The board of Kensington Steel has voted to close in December in order to give you a winter of personal struggle to forget the plant. So, in spring, demolition can go unobstructed. Remember this: that steel plant is the tax base for the community: taxes that pay for police, road maintenance, the water treatment plant, and the school system." (from Thomas Lipinski, *The Fall-Down Artist*, New York: St. Martin's Press, 1994)

2. Why and when might AAVE be used usefully in the classroom?

3. ⊞ How many slang terms can you think of for these words?

   excellent, very good

   a person who is socially inept or unsophisticated

   an attractive person

   to be drunk

   to relax

4. Visit a classroom and observe the way that women and men participate in the lesson. Does the teacher interact with both sexes in the same way?

Reflect

How do you feel ethnicity, class, and gender have shaped your identity?

Expand Your Knowledge

1. Find out about an early controversy about African-American English in schools. Research the Ann Arbor (Michigan) case.

2. Read Eckert's or Brantlinger's work on high schools and apply their findings to a high school situation that you are familiar with.

3. Read Eble (1996), summarize her general findings about college slang, and illustrate them with examples from your university.

4. Read Tannen's *You Just Don't Understand* (1990). Make two lists: one of common male speech traits and one of common

female speech traits. After reading the book, circle the traits that you feel best describe your own speech. What did you find?

5. View *American Tongues*, which is about dialects in America. Is your local dialect included? What was new to you in the film?

Suggested Readings

Lisa Delpit and Joanne Kilgour Dowdy, eds. *The Skin That We Speak. Thoughts on Language and Culture in the Classroom.* New York: The New Press, 2002.

Thomas Lipinski. *The Fall-Down Artist.* New York: St. Martin's Press, 1994.

John R. Rickford. *African American Vernacular English: Features, Evolution, Educational Implications.* Malden, MA: Blackwell, 1999.

Geneva Smitherman. *Talkin' that Talk: Language, Culture and Education in African America.* New York: Routledge, 2000.

Mary Talbot. *Language and Gender: An Introduction.* Cambridge: Polity Press, 1998.

Nonverbal Communication

1. Think of ten common gestures in your culture. What do they mean? Do you think they mean the same thing in other cultures?

2. What kinds of body language do students use to say that they like a class, are interested in a topic, dislike a class, and/or are bored?

3. ▦ Form two lines, with at least six feet between you and the person facing you. Walk toward your partner until you no longer feel comfortable. Who stopped first? What is the distance between the two of you at the end? Compare your experiences with your classmates' experiences.

Chapter 9 first returns to the question of universals and particulars using emotional facial displays as an example. The main body of the chapter will help you understand how meaning is communicated through nonverbal communication (personal space, gestures, posture, touching, eye contact, and paralanguage). It also shows how differences in nonverbal communication may cause misunderstandings. Finally, we explore the classroom consequences of differences in nonverbal communication.

Introduction

Nonverbal communication can emphasize, contradict, or substitute for verbal behavior. Nonverbal communication consists of three systems: proxemics, kinesics, and paralanguage. **Proxemics** is the study of how space is used to communicate. **Kinesics** is the study of body motion; it covers the areas of gestures, posture, touching, facial expressions, and eye contact. **Paralanguage** is concerned with the use of the voice during speech—pitch, loudness, and rate of speech, among other things.

While nonverbal communication varies to a certain degree within nationalities and groups (according to age, gender, and ethnicity), it is possible to make some general observations and contrasts. Because of globalization and increased mobility of populations, few countries have an isomorphic match to one culture. Before we survey nonverbal communication, let us once again return to the question of universals and culture-specific behavior.

Universals and Particulars:
The Case of Emotional Facial Displays

The argument for the culturally specific nature of nonverbal communication was made by Birdwhistell (1970). He took smiling as a simple example of a behavior that varies considerably even within the United States. He found that middle-class people in Ohio, Indiana, and Illinois smiled more to strangers on the street than New Englanders did. The highest incidence of smiling was found in southern cities like Atlanta, Louisville, Memphis, and Nashville. His research led him to believe that smiling is not natural but instead is a learned behavior shaped by culture.

Darwin hypothesized that there were universals in facial behaviors that conveyed each emotion. That is, humans can recognize an angry face or a sad face, no matter how different the culture background of the person displaying that face. Ekman (1982) has done extensive work to test this hypothesis. Perhaps the best evidence found for universals in displaying emotions are studies he and his colleagues did in New Guinea. Central to any research on intercultural recognition of emotions is the issue of contact and learned behavior. Americans may learn how to interpret French gestures through contact with people from France or perhaps from watching French movies. Ekman and his colleagues found members of the Fore group in New Guinea who had very little contact with Westerners. The Fore were shown three photos at a time and given a situation (e.g., the death of a child). They were asked to choose which expression would occur in each situation. The Fore agreed with the Western interpretation of the photos to a very large degree. Ninety-two percent of the Fore labeled the "happy" photo as happy, and 84 percent labeled the "angry" photo as angry. The sole exception was the photo meant to convey fear. Fear was discriminated from anger and sadness but not from surprise.

Other members of the Fore culture were asked to model the emotions called for in the judgment task *(How would you look if your child died, and you were sad?)*. They were videotaped, and the tapes were shown to U.S. college students. The students, who had never seen a person from New Guinea before, were able to accurately label the emotions, with the exception again of fear/surprise, which the Fore had trouble distinguishing. Both experiments, among others we have not mentioned, led Ekman to argue for a universal element to emotional display.

Yet there may be cultural rules for the ways that emotions are displayed. Japanese and Americans were observed watching a film that brought on stress. Both groups reacted in similar ways when observed watching the film. After the viewing, each group was interviewed by a member of its own culture. The Japanese then displayed different behavior from the Americans when discussing the effect the film had on them. Here, social rules came into play. Japanese and Americans differed on what was considered appropriate behavior when reporting their stress. Thus, it seems that there are, as Ekman argued, universals, but these universals are mitigated by social or cultural rules for the display of emotions.

Proxemics: Space and Communication

Each culture has its tacitly approved sense of personal space. Researchers have suggested that South Americans and Middle Easterners stand closer together than Americans do while conversing, though in both cases there are variations between countries in the regions. Most Asians seem to prefer a greater distance between speakers than Americans do. Much depends on the relationship between the speakers and the topic being discussed, of course.

Hall (1966) was a pioneer in the study of the communicative meaning of space. He used mostly middle-class European Americans living predominately in the northeastern part of the United States to develop a model of the use of personal space. Hall called the distance between touching and 18 inches between two people *intimate distance*. Intimate distance was considered inappropriate in public among the American adults Hall observed. He notes, however, that Russians or Middle Easterners may consider this an appropriate social distance, thereby causing considerable discomfort to Americans they may be talking to. *Personal distance* (18 inches–4 feet, for Americans, according to Hall) is the bubble people maintain around themselves. *Social distance* (4–12 feet) and personal distance have no exact boundary between them, but intimates obviously can approach personal distance while business is done at social distance (almost literally "at arm's length"). The upper bounds of social distance allow for some disengagement. Even intimates sitting in a room 10–12 feet apart will not necessarily feel the need to engage each other. One may read the paper while the other pays bills, and while either may comment or strike up a conversation, neither will feel uncomfortable ignoring the other for stretches of time. *Public dis-*

tance of more than 12 feet usually signals some formal relationship. Those who have sat in the front row of a small theater without a raised stage may have felt a certain discomfort as the public distance between them and the actors shrinks to something closer to social distance.

Kinesics: Motion and Communication

Gestures

Speakers use gestures for several different reasons. Gestures may help the speaker remember a word or help the speaker keep an idea "at hand," so to speak. Gestures may also play a role in conversation by allowing the listener to give feedback silently. They may be useful in a conversation to indicate the place and time something happened. Gestures may fill in for a word. They may indicate an entire speech act, such as a simple shrug or the southern Italian *hand purse,* which indicates *Why?* (Kendon 1997).

Gesture is a broad word that has been used for many distinct activities. McNeill (1992) presents what he calls "Kendon's continuum" of gestures. At one end is *gesticulation,* which is always accompanied by speech; gesticulation indeed helps form speech. Someone may talk about an accident and may show, simultaneous with speech, the movements of the cars involved. What McNeill calls *language-like gestures* are those that substitute for words in a sentence. Someone may say, "He's a little . . . " and finish the sentence with a movement of the hand, palm down, wrist slightly rotated back and forth, to indicate disapproval or lack of trust. Gestures like those mentioned so far are not conventionalized; individuals may not agree on the "proper" way to describe an accident or display lack of trust. *Pantomimes* too lack conventionalization, for the most part. They are characterized by a complete lack of speech. One roommate may tell another who is talking on the phone that she's going to go out and come back through pantomime. There might be more agreement among members of the culture about the best way to accomplish this than the best way to describe an accident.

Emblems are the sort of gestures that we usually mean when we use the word *gesture.* They have conventional meanings within the culture and are not accompanied by speech. Their reason for existence may in fact be to substitute for speech (often taboo speech). Another characteristic of emblems is that there is agreement on their form. The *OK* sign cannot be made with the thumb and the third finger; instead, it is made with thumb and index finger forming a circle. It's not insulting to hold up the ring finger by itself. Emblems include the head toss and the thumb held to the nose. Another emblem is the horns that the University of Texas uses as a rallying symbol and that in southern Italy mean that you consider someone a cuckold.

The end of this continuum is occupied by *sign languages*. These are very different from the other gestures, being complete, well-formed, autonomous languages (see Chapter 10).

Cultural Differences in Emblems

Cultures differ greatly in their use of emblems; this can have both amusing, inconsequential results and quite serious results for business and diplomacy. There have been several famous examples of U.S. politicians unintentionally insulting large crowds by using American gestures. President Richard Nixon in a South American trip as Vice President flashed the *OK* sign with both hands, not knowing it was an obscene, insulting gesture to his audience. They booed. President George H. W. Bush made the *V for Victory* sign as he rode in a limousine through a crowd of Australians. The trouble was his palm was facing him, not the crowd. This is an obscene gesture in Australia (and England), comparable to one made with one middle finger in the United States. Similarly the "thumbs up" gesture is considered obscene in many countries.

Most cultures have set routines for greeting others. In North America, handshakes are common. The best handshake is considered to be a firm one that does not last too long and is accompanied by looking into the other person's eyes. Both handshakes and eye contact differ significantly in other parts of the world, however. A handshake in the Arab world may not be as firm as one between two North Americans, because a firm grip is considered aggressive. In Islamic countries, men and women are generally not allowed to shake hands. In Japan and Korea, direct eye contact when greeting (or at other times) may be considered disrespectful. In South America, a handshake may be accompanied by a hug and a pat on the back. Generally, North Americans shake hands at first meeting but may not shake hands with friends. The French shake hands much more frequently than North Americans do. Something as simple as a handshake, then, turns out to be quite complex.

Not everyone shakes hands. In India and Thailand, the same gesture is used for greeting. The Indians call it a *namaste*, and the Thais call it a *wai*. It consists of putting the hands together in a prayer position, chest high. The gesture is frequently accompanied by a slight bow. The *salaam* is used by more traditional members of the older generation in the Middle East. The right hand is moved from the heart to the forehead and upward and outward.

Farewell gestures also differ. The American *good-bye* wave looks like the European and Latin American "no" gesture. In much of Europe, *good-bye* is also a wave, but the arm is extended with the palm down, not out. The hand moves at the wrist. This gesture looks quite a bit like the Japanese gesture for *come here*. The Greeks and Italians wave *good-bye* in a gesture that is familiar to Americans as *come here*—arm out, palm up, fingers curled back and forth.

In North America, nodding the head up and down generally means *yes* and shaking the head back and forth means *no*. Traditionally, in southeastern Europe (the former Yugoslavia, Bulgaria, Greece, Turkey), Iran, and parts of India, the opposite was true. Throwing the head back in Greece and southern Italy may mean *no* (but in Germany may indicate that someone wants you to come closer). In parts of India, the head toss backward means *yes*.

Posture

The way we hold our bodies is often synchronized with the way we speak. We use gestures and lean closer to our conversation partner to make points. We change our facial expressions. We often synchronize our posture with other people as a sign of our involvement in (but not necessarily agreement with) the conversation. Posture lets people know we are interested in and following the conversation.

Cultures differ in their rules for carrying the body and maintaining it at rest. The Japanese and Koreans, for example, have traditionally sat on cushions on the floor while Europeans have sat on chairs. There are rules for polite sitting on the floor and polite sitting on chairs. When sitting on the floor in a formal situation in Japan or Korea, the feet are tucked under the buttocks so that the person is sitting on the heels of the feet. When sitting formally in chairs, Japanese men and women, as is true in the United States and many other countries, cross their legs differently, and in very formal situations should not cross them at all. Around the world, it is very common to see people waiting or resting in a squatting position, with their arms resting on their knees. Such a position is less frequently seen in the United States.

Touching

We use a wide variety of actions while speaking. We pat heads and backs, shake or hold hands, hug, tickle, kiss, and maybe even pinch cheeks. When things go wrong, we may slap, punch, or kick. We may touch ourselves—shielding our eyes or ears, crossing our legs, folding our arms, straightening our clothes. A number of popular books have been written to show people what such behavior means, *how to read a person like a book.* Needless to say, it is an inexact science.

Touching is highly cultural. Experts in intercultural behavior talk about contact and non-contact cultures. In general, Americans do not, they say, appreciate being touched by strangers or even acquaintances. This is a feeling shared by most northern European cultures like those of Great Britain, Sweden, Norway, and Denmark. Other European cultures, such as those of Russia, Italy, Greece, Spain, and Portugal, are supposed to be much more comfortable with touching. Most of this talk obscures a lot of differences within cultures.

Eye Contact

Cultures differ on the appropriacy of eye contact. North American, British, Eastern European, and Saudi Arabian cultures favor eye contact. Arabs may be uncomfortable with a peripheral conversation such as one in which two people walk along side by side talking and may prefer to look at their conversational partners. Many Asian, Caribbean, and African cultures think direct or lengthy eye contact is rude or aggressive.

Paralanguage

Paralanguage is concerned with the signals we give while speaking words. The pitch level and pitch variability of our speech may signal our emotions, as may the tempo or rate of our speech and the duration we hold certain words. "I'm not angry" means different things as we change pitch or draw out *not*, for example. In fact, while the words mean one thing, the paralanguage signals may mean quite another.

Some studies have correlated vocal cues with perceptions of personality. Breathiness (think of the way Marilyn Monroe talked) is seen as a hyper-feminine speech trait in women. Flatness is usually associated with masculinity (think here of John Wayne). Nasality is, for most Americans, regarded as a socially undesirable vocal trait. In movies, nasality might signal that someone is untrustworthy. A high rate of speech is seen to convey a dynamic personality.

Paralinguistic cues like silence, backchannel behavior *(Uh huh, Umm),* and pauses help us manage conversation, giving us clues when to change speakers. (See Chapter 4.)

Classroom Nonverbal Communication

Nonverbal communication is an important element in classrooms. A lot of meaning is conveyed between students and teachers through posture, facial expression, and gestures (Neill 1991).

Teachers may convey a sense of classroom control though their posture. Dominance is often not so much a matter of a stiff appearance but a relaxed one. Children as well as adolescents are likely to perceive a teacher who fidgets as someone who is nervous or defensive. Teachers are able to communicate a sense of enthusiasm, through quick speech, smiles, and emphatic gestures. Teachers are able to convey interest in individual student questions by looks of concentration (a furrowed brow), smiles, the tilting of the head, and a forward lean.

Teachers make extensive use of two common types of gesture, what Neill (1991) calls the *iconic* and the *metaphoric.* Iconic gestures might include those that illustrate the slippage of tectonic plates during an earthquake or the movement of a column of soldiers during a battle. Metaphoric gestures might show what kind of idea is being transmitted. A cupped hand might indicate a question, or hands to the chest might show an opinion that is "held."

Intercultural misunderstandings can arise in classrooms when the cultures of students and the teacher disagree on the meanings of gestures, facial expression, and gaze. People new to teaching ESL, for example, frequently interpret widespread nodding in the class as understanding, while the students may well think they are merely indicating attention. Common American teacher behavior such as sitting on the teacher's desk is interpreted by many cultures as slovenly behavior.

Teaching Scenario

You do a classroom observation of a new ESL teacher who has a great desire to communicate with his students. While teaching, he sits on the teacher's desk or leans on the podium. When he does stand up straight, he keeps his hands in his pants pockets. Because he doesn't know the students' names yet, he calls on them by pointing with one finger. He tells you that once he does learn their first names, he will use them, and he wants them to call him by his first name. The teacher is well prepared and seems to be doing a good job. Do you see any pitfalls for him?

 ## Check Your Knowledge

1. What evidence is there for the following as human universals and as cultural artifacts?
   facial displays
   personal space
   gestures
2. What are the differences among gesticulation, pantomime, and emblem?
3. Be able to define and give examples of these terms:
   proxemics
   kinesics
   paralanguage

Apply Your Knowledge

1. Make a list of ten common gestures suitable for teaching to students learning English for the first time.
2. Assume someone is traveling to another country on business. What would you tell this person to be aware of, based on your

reading of this chapter? What questions might that person ask before leaving that would help make the trip a success?

Reflect

▦ Do you have personal experience with—or do you know any instances of—any miscommunication that has occurred due to nonverbal communication? Discuss in groups.

Expand Your Knowledge

1. Visit a classroom and observe another teacher. What kinds of gestures and body language does the teacher use in the classroom? What are the students' gestures and body language like? Does there seem to be any miscommunication occurring between the teacher and the students?

2. 🎬 Find a foreign film, and watch it with the sound off. Make a list of the gestures, and try to guess their meanings. Did you notice any gestures that were new to you or different from your own culture?

Suggested Readings

Roger E. Axtell. *Gestures: The Do's and Taboos of Body Language around the World*. 2d ed. New York: John Wily & Sons, 1998.

Jeffra Flaitz et al. *Understanding Your International Students: An Educational, Cultural, and Linguistic Guide*. Ann Arbor: University of Michigan Press, 2003.

Mark L. Knapp and Judith Hall. *Nonverbal Communication in Human Interaction*. 5th ed. Belmont, CA: Wadsworth, 2001.

Sign
Languages

Helen Keller and Anne Sullivan

1. Have you ever observed people using sign language? Can you remember any aspect of it or any impression you had?

2. ⊞ Thinking back to Chapter 2 and Chapter 9, answer these questions:
   - What is language?
   - Why would we say that sign languages are true languages and not gestures?

Chapter 10 will help you understand that sign languages are systems and true languages. As true languages, they show variation in their use. The chapter also shows that deaf culture is an important part of sign language. We conclude with a look at issues in deaf education.

Dispelling Myths

Sign language is a visual and manual form of communication that obeys the rules of natural languages. The symbols of sign language appear as signs composed of handshapes, locations, movements, and palm orientations. Signs are not gestures. Nearly all users of language can use gestures, while few can sign. As a natural language, sign language uses arbitrary signs; there is no connection in most cases between the form of the sign and its meaning. To be sure, there are some iconic signs in American Sign Language, such as those for BANANA, which looks like the action of someone peeling a banana, or MILK, which is signed by an action that looks like milking a cow. Sign languages come into existence and evolve based on the communities that use them. It follows, then, that sign languages are not understood universally. One country may have one sign language or several, depending on the history of its deaf community. In the United States, there are speakers of different kinds of sign language, to the extent that there are foreign-born deaf people living in the United States; however, the language used most commonly in the deaf community is American Sign Language (ASL). In addition, in the United States, there are also Manually Coded English systems such as Signed English, Signing Exact English, or Seeing

Essential English that attempt to replicate the word order and inflectional morphemes of English. They have had popularity in educational circles, but the Deaf (those who consider themselves culturally deaf) embrace ASL as a natural language expressing their own point of view.

Sign as a System

As do all natural languages, sign language has systems of phonology, morphology, syntax, semantics, and discourse.

While sign languages do not generally identify phonemes as units of sound, they do have an organization of phonology analogous to spoken languages. Every sign is defined by certain parameters: handshape, location, movement, and palm orientation. A change in one leads to a change in meaning, just as a *mom* is not a *mop* or a *bull* is not a *ball*. For example, the ASL signs for FATHER and MOTHER are identical in hand shape, movement, and palm orientation but differ in location.

Sign languages have morphology. Just as English uses *–er* at the end of a verb to indicate the agent (a worker is one who works), ASL uses a manual suffix referred to as an *agent marker*.

Many spoken languages rely on word order to convey information about subjects and objects. English, for example, puts the subject before the object in declarative statements. ASL has basically (with some exceptions) the same word order as English: S-V-O. English word order usually helps the listener know whether a statement or question has been made (*The dog is sleeping. Is the dog sleeping?*), though we do also use rising intonation to ask a question (*You coming with us?*). Sign languages use non-manual signals such as facial expressions (e.g., raised eyebrows) and posture to differentiate types of utterances.

Sign languages are independent of the spoken languages of the communities in which they are used. There is lexical borrowing, however, and words that get borrowed are usually encoded in the writing system of the spoken language. Thus, ASL borrows words from English through the manual alphabet or fingerspelling. There is a one-handed sign for each of the 26 English letters. People's names, for examples, are spelled, at least when used initially.

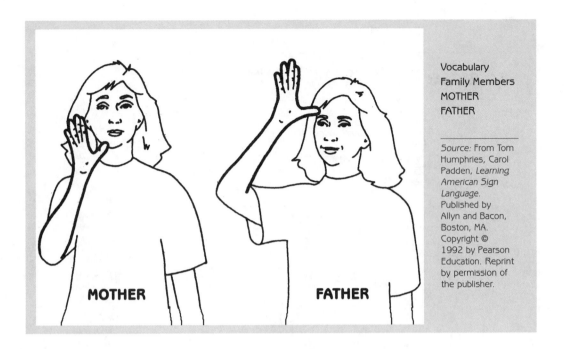

Vocabulary
Family Members
MOTHER
FATHER

Source: From Tom Humphries, Carol Padden, *Learning American Sign Language*. Published by Allyn and Bacon, Boston, MA. Copyright © 1992 by Pearson Education. Reprint by permission of the publisher.

MOTHER   FATHER

Variation in Sign Languages

Estimates of the number of sign languages in the world are confusing. The Ethnologue database maintained by the Summer Institute of Linguistics lists 114 sign languages. This number is probably low, given that it represents only languages that have been described by linguists. The issue of whether a variety is a language or a dialect figures in counting sign languages, just as it does in counting spoken languages. Some researchers, for example, have claimed that South Africa has one sign language with some lexical variation but mutual intelligibility across dialects, while other researchers claim that there are in fact up to 12 separate sign languages in the country. Differences in sign languages often do not match differences in languages spoken within the same area. Very often, the variety of sign language used has been most influenced by the nationalities of the people who set up the schools for the deaf. For example, French sign language had an early effect on ASL because the first teacher at the first permanent school for the deaf in the United States was French. Colonialism has also had an effect on the variety of sign language chosen. Some dialects of Taiwan's sign language show influence of the Japanese occupation, while others show the influence of immigrants from Shanghai (Woll, Sutton-Spence, and Elton 2001).

store   The store opens at 10:00 a.m. Monday through Saturday.

1 Alabama, California, Colorado, Florida, Illinois, Kentucky, Louisiana, Massachusetts (1 of 2), Michigan, Missouri, New Mexico, New York, North Carolina (1 of 2), North Dakota, Ohio, Pennsylvania (1 of 3), Texas, Utah, Washington, Wisconsin
2 Arkansas
3 Hawaii
4 Maine
5 Massachusetts (2 of 2)
6 North Carolina (2 of 2)
7 Pennsylvania (2 of 3)
8 Pennsylvania (3 of 3)
9 South Carolina, Virginia

Source: Signs across America by Edgar H. Shroyer and Susan P. Shroyer.

As natural languages, sign languages vary. Some of the factors involved in sign language variation are geography, age, ethnicity, gender, religion, and socioeconomic status, in short, all the factors that lead to variation in spoken languages. Variation is manifested in lexical items, phonology, and grammar. Different groups use different signs for certain words or change the sign slightly. There is variation, for example, in the use of signs made on the hand versus signs made on the face and variation in the use of one-handed and two-handed forms of the same sign (Lucas et al. 2001).

Conversation

ASL discourse also has rules of conversation. (Not all of its discourse rules are like those of spoken languages.) People take orderly turns. One signal that the conversation has come to a *turn relevance place* (a place where the subject of the conversation may be changed) is when hands are at rest in the group. A signer might raise the hands to bid for the floor, the turn to sign. There are many possible ways for someone to get the floor, however, including shifts in posture or head movement, eye gaze, and tapping on the shoulder to get someone's attention. Discourse in ASL is marked by overlaps, as all conversations are.

Cohesion in discourse is marked by both discourse markers like *then* and by the use of space. The signer may establish a spatial position for a referent like a city or person early on in the conversation. Subsequent references to that place or person will be made in that signed space. A person's mother, for instance, may be set up on the left side of the signing space in front of the signer, and the father set up on the right side. As the conversation continues, those spaces will be used to refer back to each individual (Metzger and Bahan 2001).

Deaf Culture

The Deaf Community in the United States and English-speaking Canada is linked by a shared language, ASL, and (somewhat controversially) a shared culture, which Deaf people have created, changed, and transmitted. Within the Deaf community, there are a number of differences based on geography, ethnicity, class, and race, to be sure, and what follows is only a generalized sketch.

The question of culture in the Deaf community is an interesting one. Not all Deaf people consider themselves culturally Deaf. Many Deaf people claim membership in a unique Deaf culture. There are some hearing people, primarily those raised by Deaf parents, who belong to the Deaf culture. *Deaf* also takes in a wide range of hearing abilities. In the past, residential schools played a large part in the formulation of Deaf identity, but changes in school funding in recent years have led to more children being educated not in boarding schools but in public schools nearer their homes. Some hearing children are raised Deaf. Padden and Humphries (1988) tell of a boy raised on a farm by a Deaf family who didn't know he was hearing until he was six. He obviously could hear, but hearing was in a sense meaningless to him. They point out how much things depend on what you conceive of as the center of your world. They show how the sign HEARING has the denotation *can hear*, but it is related to DEAF in interesting ways. HARD-OF-HEARING in both ASL and English means *a deviation of some kind*. The similarities stop there, at least among some ASL users. To some Deaf people, A-LITTLE-HARD-Of-HEARING refers to someone who is close to deaf (has only a little hearing), while VERY-HARD-OF-HEARING is far from deaf and hears well. Of course, from the English speaker's point of view, things are reversed, and some ASL users may indeed accept English's meaning and give these signs their English connotation. Padden and Humphries also tell the story of a football game between two Deaf schools in which the spectators referred to the football players and their fans on the opposing side by signing HEARING (not us). Here, the students were claiming an identity based on their shared Deafness (even though the other team shared that Deafness).

Those who are deaf, when given the opportunity, can fit very well into their communities. Groce (1985) reports on the hereditary deaf community of Martha's Vineyard, an island off the coast of Massachusetts. From the 1700s to the 1950s, there was a significant deaf population in one area of the island. The non-deaf population simply learned sign language in order to communicate with their neighbors. The deaf were not seen as limited in any way, but as full members of society.

A seminal event in Deaf culture occurred in 1988 with a large protest at Gallaudet University, the only world's university for the Deaf. The protest began when the Board of Trustees selected a hearing president. Gallaudet, in fact, had never, in its then 124-year history, had a deaf president. After a week of protests, the chair of the board and the new president both resigned and a deaf dean of the university was appointed the new president (Sacks 1989).

Deaf Education in the United States

Thomas Hopkins Gallaudet established the first permanent school for the deaf in Hartford, Connecticut, in 1817. The first teacher was Laurent Clerc, a deaf French man. The language of instruction was a form of signed English adapted from signed French. The language of the dormitories was an early form of ASL. A relatively high percent of early teachers of the deaf were themselves deaf, so ASL probably also found its way into some classrooms at some times.

By 1860, calls had begun for using oralism at deaf schools, that is, for teaching students who had some hearing to speak rather than sign, or at least for supporting signing with speech. The educational reformer Horace Mann was at the forefront of importing oral approaches from Europe, and the inventor of the telephone, Alexander Graham Bell, was a strong advocate for the reforms in the United States. As the 19th century continued, oral-only schools were established. Gallaudet's son, Edward Miner Gallaudet, advocated tailoring the approach to the child, teaching lip reading and oral skills where possible. By the end of the 19th century, oralism was firmly established as the preferred method, and most residential schools were oral until the 1960s.

As research on ASL advanced in the 1960s, there was growing acceptance of it, but the decade also saw the growth of other manual approaches such as Signed English, Seeing Essential English (SEE1), and Signing Exact English (SEE2), particularly as a way to teach reading and writing in English. Deaf community leaders continued to advocate for ASL. This time also saw the rise of the Total Communication approach, which in practice often adopted the notion of Simultaneous Communication, or signing while speaking.

Literacy is especially important because ASL does not yet have a widely used writing system. In fact, a typical deaf U.S. high school graduate reads at the fourth-grade level and, as a non-native user of English, makes errors in writing like omitting or using incorrect articles, prepositions, and verb tense markers. Literacy problems such as these can keep deaf workers in low-paying jobs. Many approaches to ESL literacy development for ASL users use whole-language approaches as well as video input to writing tasks.

More recently, researchers and practitioners have argued that Deaf education should take the form of bilingual education in ASL and English. Classes can be used to maintain ASL as the first language, while ASL is used to teach academic subjects, oral communication skills, and English literacy. Bilingual education builds upon the child's linguistic resources in ASL. Concepts transfer from ASL to English while ASL remains a valuable source of identity and self-esteem.

ASL as a Foreign Language

ASL is taught at high schools and universities as a foreign language. That is, it satisfies the graduation requirement that students study another language. Initial reactions to the proposal that ASL be substituted for Spanish or French were frequently hostile. It took years in some cases to convince people that ASL is a language. The *foreign* part of the phrase *foreign language* was also a matter of debate. ASL is, after all, indigenous to the United States. Several indigensous languages, like Navajo, are accepted for foreign language credit. Speakers of heritage languages like Spanish may receive credit for learning the standard dialect of their home language. Perhaps the best argument, however, is that the purpose of learning a foreign language is to acquaint students with another culture and, as we have seen, ASL indeed has its own vibrant culture. Unfortunately, students often enter ASL classes thinking they are going to have an easy time. It turns out that you need to study ASL just as hard as you would Spanish or French.

Teaching Scenario

A deaf child enters third grade in your school. She seems to be reading below grade level. Why is intervention especially important?

☑ Check Your Knowledge

1. Think about your answer to #1 in Before You Read. Do you have anything to add to your answer?
2. What is the difference between ASL and systems like Signed English?
3. How are phonology and morphology realized in ASL?
4. Do sign languages vary? How?
5. What are some models of Deaf education?

Apply Your Knowledge

1. Consult an ASL dictionary. Learn ten signs of your choice.
2. Compare the signs in the first question with how words are presented in one of the Manually Coded English systems.

Reflect

What does the controversy over how to teach deaf children say about our attitudes toward language in general? About parents and children? About education?

Expand Your Knowledge

1. Watch *Children of a Lesser God,* and report on it.
2. Research your own local deaf community. What is done to educate deaf children in your community?
3. Research regional variation in ASL. Find variations for ten signs across the United States.

Suggested Readings

Nora Groce. *Everybody Here Spoke Sign Language: Hereditary Deafness on Martha's Vineyard*. Cambridge: Harvard University Press, 1985.

Carol Padden and Tom Humphries. *Deaf in America: Voices from a Culture*. Cambridge: Harvard University Press, 1988.

Literacy

1. What are the differences between speech and writing?

2. What do you remember about learning to read? To write?

3. ⊞ Is the language of e-mail and the Internet writing or speech? What makes you say so?

Chapter 11 will help you understand issues in literacy. We first question the differences between speech and writing. We then outline controversies in the study of orality and literacy and present some educational implications of differences in literacy, including bilingual literacy. We then show that writing is socially constructed and introduce the ideas of genre, discourse community, and contrastive rhetoric before concluding with a look at differences in scripts and writing systems.

Speech and Writing

The modern linguistic tradition once took speech to be virtually synonymous with language. In the first half of the last century, writing was taken to be a pale, theoretically uninteresting reflection of language. Over the past 20 years, however, more attention has been paid to written language. One strain of that research has looked at the differences between speech and writing. Speech and writing have been characterized, at least in English, as differing in

- *complexity:* Writing is more complex. Sentences are longer than in speech. Subordinate clauses are used more frequently in writing than in speech.
- *explicitness and context:* Writers have the obligation to lead the reader through the text, clearly signposting ideas and transitions, and making connections and assumptions explicit. Speakers in a conversation, on the other hand, assume lots of shared information.
- *amount of information:* Writing tends to pack in more information than conversation does.

- *organization:* Writing is planned and casual speech isn't.
- *involvement:* Writing is detached; conversation is involved.

The rise of electronic discourse, computer-mediated communication (CMC), or what Crystal (2001) calls *Netspeak* has brought the issue of speech versus writing to the fore again. Is the language of the Internet more like writing or more like speech—or is it something in between, a new hybrid of speech and language? It depends on where you are looking. Web pages are often little more than archived writing, yet when interactivity is introduced to a website, in the form of e-mail, for example, elements of speech may be introduced. Websites often are, however, not as permanent as a book; they may change appearance or content or even disappear. E-mail and chatgroups share certain elements of face-to-face communication; people often try to write in an informal way, as if they were speaking. Nevertheless, standard elements of speech like backchanneling *(Uh huh)* and paralinguistic features (facial expression, gestures, and intonation) are all missing in electronic discourse. Computer-mediated discourse can seem abrupt and cold compared to a conversation. Thus, people feel the need to use *emoticons* like ;-) (for a wink) or notations such as <g> (for a grin) in order to make their meaning clear.

Biber (1988) called all these assumptions about speech and writing into question by measuring the distribution of certain linguistic features in speech and writing in different kinds of text. His analysis showed that there is no single feature that clearly discriminates between speaking and writing. Different genres show different results. Both conversation and personal letters show a high degree of involvement. Academic writing is abstract, but novels are not. Biber concludes that the differences lie in text types, not in the modes of speech and writing.

Thus, speech and writing can be investigated using many of the same techniques. Basso (1989), for example, has shown that an "ethnography of writing" can be researched using the familiar framework of the ethnography of speaking.

One aspect of electronic discourse we have not touched upon is the increased need for learners to be literate in reading images as well as in reading print. Kress (2003) argues that "language-as-writing" will be replaced in many cases by images; in short, there will be a "move from *telling the world* to *showing the world.*" In Kress's view, writing is organized sequentially, over time, and images are organized simultaneously, through space, so the ways in which we interact with each are different. Kress is a member of the New London Group, which is made up of researchers who have called for a pedagogy of literacy that takes into account both the diversity of voices within post-modern societies and the influence of multimedia on literacy.

Orality and Literacy

Ong (1982) made much (as we will see, probably too much) of the difference between orality and literacy. Ong synthesized and extended a wide range of scholarship on the differences between oral and literate cultures. He claimed that the introduction of literacy led to changes in thought. As part of his evidence, he used the research of Luria (1976) among literate and non-literate people in remote areas of Uzbekistan and Kyrgyzstan in the early 1930s. Luria showed how those with even some literacy answered his questions differently than those who could not read or write. The non-literate thought situationally; when presented with a hammer, bucket, saw, and log, they chose the bucket as the thing that did not belong to the group (hammers and saws are tools to work wood). A schooled person grouped the three tools together. When asked to complete a syllogism, *Northern countries have white bears. Novaya Zembla is a northern country. What color are its bears?* the non-literate protested that they had never been there and could not say; each place has its own animals. Requests for definitions or generalizations such as *What is a tree?* were met with incredulity by the non-literate; everyone knows what a tree is.

Ong claimed that the mental world of a person in an oral culture is engaged with the surroundings and is not objectively distanced. Written language changes the way people think because it is context free. Writing does not just change how individuals think, but it was ultimately, according to Ong, transformative of human consciousness.

Careful readers will note that in one case we used *literate* and *schooled* as synonymous when talking about Luria's experiments. Indeed, Luria, fairly enough, took the two to be synonymous. Gee (1996) points out that in fact schooling is much more than literacy. Children (even university students) learn roles to play in school, procedures to follow, genres to write in, and values to hold. Scribner and Cole (1981) investigated the effects of schooling and three types of literacy among the Vai people of Liberia. The Vai acquired English literacy in school but also had an indigenous script used for commercial recordkeeping and for letterwriting. They, in addition, as Muslims, used Arabic to read and memorize the Quran. Some people were literate in all three scripts, some in none, and others in one or two. If literacy alone led to a different way of thinking, it shouldn't matter which script was used. Scribner and Cole used tasks like those used by Luria. Neither Arabic nor the indigenous script, both acquired outside formal schooling, had an effect on classification tasks or the ability to complete syllogisms. Only the schooled literacy, English, had some effect on abstract thinking, and that effect was the ability to talk about the tasks, to explain why they were done as they were (in essence, to explain what a tree is, to return to Luria's question). The English-schooled subjects did no better on the tasks themselves. The factor that did seem to separate people was urban living. People who lived in cities, for example, did better at classification tasks.

Scribner and Cole propose a "practice theory of literacy." Certain types of literacy may have an effect on certain kinds of skills. Those literate in the indigenous Vai script did well on tasks such as remembering and repeating Vai syllables and in tests of Vai grammar, but the effects of literacy were not global or transferable.

Street (1995) criticizes Ong for confusing the social contexts in which literacy operates with literacy itself. Ong seems to be describing the Western academic culture to which he belonged as he formulated the characteristics of literacy. Street also believes that Ong made too clear a separation between orality and literacy. Even in the highly literate culture of the university, orality plays a part in lectures and seminars.

Literacy, then, is not a unitary phenomenon and has a social as well as an individual or cognitive dimension. A social approach would take into account the types of literacy events and literacy practices that occur within the society or culture. It would also look at the social relations implicit in literacy practices. For example, literacy may be gendered. Is it the "job" of the husband or wife to write the checks and pay the bills within a family, and is this pattern true across the culture? Who communicates with the teacher in notes, the father or mother? Literacy may be age specific; who fixes problems with the home computer, the parents or children? Different classes and occupations may have different literacy practices. To be sure, traditions of literacy practice may not be completely clear and differentiated. Duranti and Ochs (1996) develop the notion of **syncretic literacy** to describe ways in which multiple literacy traditions may exist in the same multilingual family. In their case study, Samoan immigrants in the United States utilized both Samoan and American traditions during one small literacy event: the completion of a homework assignment.

Gregory and Williams (2000) show how *syncretic literacy*, the blending of home and school literacy practices, has occurred and continues to occur in the East End of London. They argue against any understanding of home literacies as "deprivation" and show how, for example, lessons in Quranic classes and school classes both contribute to British-Bangladeshi children's literacy.

Orality and Literacy at Home and at School

Shirley Brice Heath's classic ethnography (1983) also calls into account any sharp distinction between orality and literacy. She shows how the two interact in several communities, and how there is a mismatch between literacy expectations in some communities and literacy expectations in schools. In the 1970s, Heath lived among three communities in the Carolina Piedmont, the plateau between the Appalachian mountains and the coastal plains: Roadville, a white, working-class mill community; Trackton, an African-American, working-class mill community; and Gateway, a middle-class, urban community that included African Americans and whites. Heath looked at how each community used literacy and, in particular, how children acquired literacy and language.

People in Roadville valued personal stories, stories told about themselves or their friends in which the main character is the butt of the joke. These stories often had a moral lesson to teach. Roadville people often used personal stories to interpret biblical passages. Children in Roadville were read to at a young age; most of the books used were nursery rhymes, alphabet books, or other picture books. Some were simplified Bible stories or fairy tales. Though children did not often get to tell stories in the family, when they did, they were encouraged to tell the truth; stories having fictional characters or plots were discouraged, and fiction in general was equated with "lies." Before entering school, Roadville children had little experience with fiction. Parents also did not encourage children to make connections between what they read and the outside world. Thus, children had some difficulty in school with decontextualized knowledge and with applying knowledge gained in one area with other circumstances.

The Trackton community had a rich oral tradition. There were not the same concerns as in Roadville about "lies." A good story in Trackton was a creative one. Children were encouraged to use their imaginations and seek connections in their story telling. The stories were seldom along the formulaic lines of *Once upon a time. . . .* Indeed, children were seldom read bedtime stories. Once in school, the children's style of narrative did not match the teacher's idea of what "good" narrative was. The children also tended not to do well at the sort of reading comprehension questions found at the end of reading passages.

Reading in Trackton was usually done in a public group. Older children taught younger "what something says" on trips to the store. Adults read the newspaper aloud on the front porch as others commented. Reading in Roadville was done in groups and individually. While in Trackton, adults read to each other, in Roadville, parents read to children but only children read to adults. However, Heath claims that more people talked about reading than actually read for an extended amount of time; reading was endorsed as a good thing to do, but not much actual reading was done.

The uses of literacy Heath found in Roadville and Trackton led her to question Ong's dichotomy, as we have seen. She saw aspects of both oral and literate cultures in each group. What seemed clear to her, however, was that neither community used literacy in the way schools did.

In Gateway, the middle-class community, school-based literacy was part of children's lives almost from the beginning. Nursery walls were decorated with letters and storybook characters. There was lots of reading and talk about reading. Parents read for pleasure as well as for information. When children from Trackton and Roadville went to school, they were taught by teachers with the expectations of Gateway. The mill children had to learn new ways of telling stories and new ways of talking about stories with adults. Heath closes her book by showing how by learning some of the style of the mill communities, teachers could help children be more successful in school.

Since Heath wrote *Ways with Words*, the number of family literacy programs has grown rapidly. Family literacy programs attempt to address what are perceived to be mismatches between mainstream literacy taught in schools and literacy as it is experienced in homes. It is generally agreed that parental involvement in early literacy has a positive effect on children's knowledge about language and on motivation to read. Intervention programs have been designed to help parents to give early literacy experiences at home. Some of these efforts have been based on a top-down, we-know-best model. Moll and his colleagues have argued that families contain **funds of knowledge** that should be tapped into when designing literacy programs (Moll and Gonzalez 1994). That is, the schools should take time to investigate, as Heath did, the ways literacy happens in given communities and use that information to bridge home and school. (For a review of issues in family literacy, see Purcell-Gates 2000.)

Reading across Cultures

We have already encountered the concepts script and schema. When we read, we make use of prior knowledge through **scripts** or **schema**. Thus, when we read information in a foreign language, or even information about another culture, we are likely to bring our own cultural knowledge to that text.

It is relatively easy to show the effects of schema on reasoning by focusing on memory processes. Bartlett (1932) showed how memory is organized around story summaries. He presented a Native American story, 'The War of Ghosts," to those from outside the culture and then later asked his subjects to re-tell the story. They tended to distort the unfamiliar parts of the story in the re-telling, especially the parts involving ghosts, who were originally presented quite matter-of-factly. The subjects altered the story to conform to their beliefs and experiences and the stories they were familiar with.

Steffensen and her colleagues (1979) conducted an experiment in which two groups, natives of India and the United States, read letters describing typical weddings in each country. As expected, each group read the letter about its own wedding faster and recalled more ideas from the letter in a subsequent test. There were interesting distortions when the subjects recalled the passages. For example, an Indian subject recalled the section of the American letter that focused on the tradition of the bride wearing "something old, something new, something borrowed, and something blue" as "the dress was too old and out of fashion," perhaps because a premium is put in Indian weddings on the bride wearing a stylish *sari*. American subjects were confused by the Indian custom of the dowry, given to the groom's family by the bride's family. Some remembered the dowry as a two-way exchange, and others remembered it as party favors. We try to push our understandings about others into our own preconceived categories.

Bilingual Literacy

In the early 1960s, UNESCO (the United Nations Educational, Scientific, and Cultural Organization) saw literacy as the key for economic and social development in the new nations coming into being from the ashes of colonialism. The focus was on functional literacy, the ability to do simple tasks such as read road signs, medicine bottles, and schedules, and sign one's name. Literacy was seen as a technical skill. Critics led by Paulo Freire (1970/2000) noted this approach tended to maintain the status quo. Freire argued the necessity for critical literacy that would make people aware of their society, their disadvantaged place in it, and the possibility of political and social change.

The impact of colonialism is still being felt in literacy education. Countries in Africa, for example, continue to debate whether to make children initially literate in the old colonial languages of French or English, or in the children's home languages. Senegal teaches children to read in French, ignoring the home languages (though there have been a small number of experiments in beginning literacy in Wolof, the lingua franca). The medium of instruction in Zimbabwe's schools is English, but the government allows rural schools to teach the first years of elementary school in the local languages, Shona and Ndebele (Baker 1998). Part of the debate centers on utilitarian concerns: French and English have widespread uses, while the countries' indigenous languages may either be limited geographically or limited in the amount of material printed in them. Indeed, some languages remain unwritten, while others have acquired a writing system but only recently enough so that printed material is confined to a small number of newspapers or pamphlets.

Wagner (1993) offers a detailed look at literacy in Morocco. Morocco has three languages: Arabic, Berber, and French. Arabic is the most commonly spoken language. Berber is the indigenous language of the country; Berber monolinguals are found mostly in rural areas. French remains the language of some of the elite. Of course, many people are bilingual or trilingual.

French is only now giving way to Arabic as the language of literacy. French is taught as a second or third language beginning in the third grade of elementary school, and French is also an important language of instruction in high school and in the university. The official language of Morocco is Standard Arabic, which is based on the classical Arabic of the Quran. People speak Moroccan Arabic, a dialect of Arabic. Berber is an unwritten language, and the small number of Berber publications are transliterated into Arabic or Roman scripts.

Preschool in Morocco frequently takes the form of Quranic schools. Berber- and Arabic-speaking children both begin learning Standard Arabic, spoken and written, in these schools. While Arabic-speaking children are learning a new dialect of Arabic and literacy, Berber children are learning a new language and literacy simultaneously. Elementary school then consists of five years, taught in standard Arabic, except for eight hours of French per week taught during the last three years.

Wagner studied the literacy acquisition of children in rural Morocco. He found that Arabic-speaking children did better at reading Arabic than did Berber-speaking children during the first year of elementary school. Over time, however, the Berber children caught up with their Arabic-speaking peers, so that, by the end of elementary school, there were no significant differences in test scores between the two groups. Thus, there was some initial advantage in learning to read in the home language. Berber-speaking children who attended Quranic schools had an advantage over Berber speakers who did not; the former group more quickly reached the performance level of the Arabic speakers.

Once the children began to learn French, better readers in Arabic were better readers in French; this was true of both Arabic- and Berber-speaking students. First-literacy skills transfer to second- and third-literacy skills. This is remarkable because not only are the three languages completely unrelated, French and Arabic differ completely in their writing systems as well, down to the direction of the script, which in French is written left to right and in Arabic is written right to left.

Wagner points out that the Moroccan situation is somewhat different from that of other countries in that there is no competing literacy in Berber, because it remains unwritten; families who want their children to become literate and advance economically must support Arabic literacy. There is also great motivation to read Arabic because it is the language of the Quran. Finally, Wagner points out that spoken Moroccan Arabic is finding its way into rural areas, not yet completely replacing Berber but allowing Berber children to hear and use Arabic outside the classroom. All of these factors lead to the potential for success in language and literacy learning.

Scollon and Scollon (1981) argued that, in the case of the Athabaskan people of Alaska and Canada, writing in English, their second language, caused a loss of ethnic identity. Athabaskan discourse patterns did not easily allow for speaking or writing from a position of authority, as is demanded in English academic prose. Athabaskan discourse patterns also did not allow for the ignoring of context in favor of the idealized, autonomous text characteristic of English essayist literacy. Thus, it was difficult for Athabaskans, as Athabaskans, to write easily about their culture in school-approved English ways. Writing in English caused internal conflict in bilinguals. The implications for bilingual education are obvious; if the Scollons are correct, schooling that is not sensitive to first language discourse patterns forces a choice between ethnic identity and biliteracy.

Writing as Socially Constructed

Just as there are rules for speaking in a given discourse community, there are rules for writing, and not just of the sort that tell us to capitalize the first word of a sentence or to have a thesis statement in an argumentative essay. Purves and Hawisher (1990), for example, said that a central finding of the worldwide International Study of Written Composition in the 1980s was that good writing is culturally defined. Bohannan (1966) showed how what she had perceived to be the universal attributes of a good story may in fact be very culturally determined as she recounted her efforts to tell the Hamlet story to skeptical Tiv elders in west Africa.

One set of rules is captured by the notion of **genre**. Swales (1990) has been very influential in the thinking on genre analysis. Though most of Swales's work has been concerned with written genres such as the scientific research report, he has also applied his ideas to oral genres such as academic presentations. Swales defines genre as "a class of communicative events, the members of which share some set of communicative purpose . . . recognized by the expert members of the parent discourse community." Communicative events include not only the language produced, the discourse, but a whole set of assumptions and associations about the role of that discourse in that culture at that time. Defining genre membership in terms of purpose rather than shared characteristics underlines the idea that genres exist to achieve goals. This is a social definition of genre, one not concerned with enumerating stylistic features in isolation but in giving prominence to the discourse community. Swales provides a clear set of characteristics that allows the identification of a **discourse community**, which is, by and large, a special interest group.

A discourse community has agreed-upon goals; it communicates among its members in active ways that allow feedback; it utilizes one or more genres and specific vocabulary; it has a changing membership but maintains a suitable blend of experts and novices within its ranks. Thus, a stamp club is Swales's representative discourse community. Many researchers have stretched Swales's definition and called classrooms "discourse communities." Swales emphasizes the voluntary nature of discourse communities; "a discourse community recruits its members by persuasion, training, or relevant qualification" (1990). We would have to question on this basis the use of his definition to describe public school classrooms. Scientists and other academics, of course, do belong to discourse communities. Part of graduate school education is making novices aware of the respective genres of these communities.

Another influential tradition of research that has investigated the social nature of writing has been **contrastive rhetoric**. Kaplan (1966) began the field of contrastive rhetoric by asserting that *rhetoric,* the preferred organizational structure of text, varies from culture to culture. Just because someone can write an essay in the native language does not mean that writer is able, without training, to write an essay in a second language. Indeed, teachers of international students in American universities frequently comment that accurate sentences do not necessarily add up to a cohesive, well-organized essay. Kaplan went on to show, through examples from a number of writers, how he believed different cultures organize essays in different ways.

Kaplan characterized English expository writing in paragraphs as being organized in a relatively straightforward fashion, with a topic sentence and linear development. "Semitic" writing (Arabic and Hebrew) was characterized by parallel development, that is, by addition and coordination rather than by subordination of ideas in dependent clauses. This was conceptualized graphically as a zigzag pattern of parallel arrows. The "Oriental" (what we would now call Asian) pattern was seen as largely circular. Romance languages such as French and Spanish were said to allow for more digressions, specifically by commenting on peripheral ideas.

Kaplan was careful to say he was not assigning a value to one system over another but only pointing out the differences that might lead to problems as students tried to be successful in American universities. He proposed a series of exercises for teaching English expository text structure. Kaplan (1987) acknowledged that his 1966 conclusions were perhaps too strong and said that

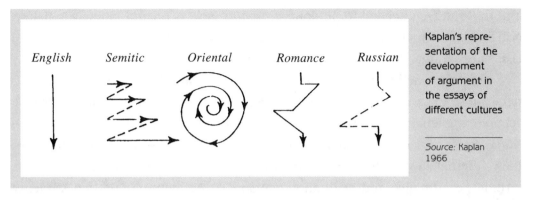

Kaplan's representation of the development of argument in the essays of different cultures

Source: Kaplan 1966

we each, as native speakers of a given language, control a number of rhetorical patterns. He, however, brought the discussion back to pedagogy, maintaining that it is the teacher's responsibility to make students aware of the possible variations in writing, their meanings, and their acceptability in given circumstances. Kaplan's work has been both extended and criticized, but the field of contrastive rhetoric continues to provide insights for pedagogy.

Hinds (1987) developed a typology that has been influential. He suggested that languages differ in the amount of responsibility they give to the speaker or writer versus the amount of responsibility they give to the listener or reader. In English, for example, the speaker or writer has more responsibility for effective communication and for being clear. In Japanese, the listener or reader has more responsibility for effective communication and must construct the meaning of the exchange. The pedagogical implication is that teaching only that there are different ways to organize essays is probably not enough, that students may profit from a discussion of ways to think about the writing process itself. Hinds (1990) later termed this reliance on the reader to make sense of what is written a "quasi-inductive" style. He expanded his 1987 conclusions about Japanese to include Korean, Chinese, and Thai languages.

There have been a number of criticisms of contrastive rhetoric research. Early criticism centered on the fact that researchers were looking at essays as only products, not processes. That is, researchers were not getting an understanding of how writers made the decisions they made or why they made them. A corollary to this argument was that Kaplan's prescriptions to teach the conventions of English essays were not well integrated into new teaching approaches that were process oriented and centered on writing to real audiences (Matsuda 1997). Another criticism was that researchers were not comparing similar texts in two languages, that is, that genres had to be taken account of and that research needed to be done in first as well as second languages. These criticisms, and more, and the subsequent research that responded to the criticisms are summarized in Connor (1996) and Grabe and Kaplan (1996).

From the standpoint of language and culture, research in contrastive rhetoric needs to be expanded in at least two directions: toward a focus on learner's first school experiences and toward an accommodation with the notion of international Englishes. Purves and Hawisher (1990) say that students and teachers have internal models based on school experiences that have an influence on writing performance and evaluation. Carson (1992) reminds us that students bring with them to second language classes not only another language but a set of beliefs about what it means to be literate and how classrooms should be organized to properly teach people to be literate. Students also bring ideas of what the purpose of writing in school should in fact be (Liebman 1992). Pedagogical techniques, such as group work, that would seem to be standard across cultures, in fact, operate in very different ways depending on the culture. The purpose of a Chinese classroom group is to help the group, while the purpose of an American classroom group is to help the individual learn (Carson and Nelson 1996). We need to know more about how students learn to write in their first language, in what situations, through what techniques, and for what reasons.

The globalization of English also presents opportunities for more research. Many have argued that what Kaplan called the English expository style is now being widely taught in secondary schools across the world. Kirkpatrick (1997) looked at recent Chinese composition textbooks and found that many were not teaching the traditional Chinese style but were instead teaching a more Western style of rhetoric. In fact, Scollon and Scollon (1981), more than 20 years ago, argued that English essayist literacy was virtually synonymous with the modern consciousness.

With many Englishes in the world, the idea of ownership of "English" rhetoric naturally arises. Critics such as Kachru (1999) see the contrastive rhetoric hypothesis as implicitly normative. Kachru argues that users of world Englishes and nonnative users of English should not have to change their identities to conform to an idealized form of American academic English.

An aspect of academic English that has been extensively commented on is plagiarism. There has been some concern that English language learners from countries with different rules about academic plagiarism are at a disadvantage in North American universities, where codes of student conduct routinely call for dismissal for the first offense. Some cultures admit, and indeed require, a greater amount of (often direct, unattributed) quotation in academic writing than is common in North American settings. Many feel it is the academy that should adapt by recognizing that plagiarism is a culturally defined concept. Others feel that it is the responsibility of English for Academic Purposes professionals to make learners aware of the differences.

Writing Systems and Scripts

Scripts have no logical connections to the languages that use them. Hebrew script is used to write both Hebrew, a Semitic language, and Yiddish, a Germanic language. Arabic script is used to write Arabic, a Semitic language, and Persian, an Indo-European language, and was used to write Turkish, an Altaic language, until the late 1920s. The languages of the central Asian republics that were formerly a part of the Soviet Union have been written in Arabic, Cyrillic, and Roman scripts, and discussion continues on which to use in the future. Religion has had some influence on script use. Cyrillic is used to write Russian, Bulgarian, and Serbian, all spoken in countries where the Eastern Orthodox Church has been powerful. The Roman alphabet is used by Poles, Czechs, and Croats in countries that have been traditionally Roman Catholic. Historically, there have been a number of different writing systems, but we will focus here on three main types: alphabetic, logographic, and syllabic.

Right now, you are reading in an alphabetic script variously called Roman, Latin, or Greco-Roman. It derives from the Phoenician script. English uses 26 letters to represent many more sounds, so we term our orthographic system *opaque* (not easily seen through). Other languages have a much more *transparent* orthographic system; the Spanish and Finnish languages are usually cited as having a near-perfect match between their sounds and the symbols in which they are written. Hebrew and Arabic are also written in alphabets, but the writing of both languages uses a system of consonant roots, with the vowels reduced to small diacritical marks that are not always used.

Chinese is the lone *logographic* script in the world. Each morpheme in Chinese is a character composed of from 1 to more than 20 strokes of the pen. (For this reason, some scholars prefer to call Chinese not logographic but morpho-syllabic.) The characters, called *Hanzi* in China, *Hancha* in Korea, and *Kanji* in

Japan, have been a unifying cultural force in east Asia for centuries. Because Chinese culture was so prestigious, Korea and Japan borrowed Chinese characters to write their own (very different) languages. In fact, written Chinese serves to unify the separate languages of China. A person from the south of China generally will not be able to understand a person from the north, but they can write each other notes using characters and understand each other perfectly (though their individual pronunciations of the characters would be different if they pronounced them aloud). Similarly, Japanese and Chinese people can communicate with each other in writing though their languages are completely different (and though reform efforts in each country have simplified the characters in different ways). Older Koreans could communicate in the same way; however, the South Korean educational system and the country at large has been de-emphasizing characters; high school students still learn about 1,800 of them (Taylor 1998). A comprehensive historical dictionary of Chinese would have about 50,000 characters. The average Chinese high school student would know about 3,000 characters. A high school graduate in Japan should know the 1,945 characters listed by the Ministry of Education; a typical adult would know probably at least one thousand more. The most frequent misconception about characters is that they are pictures. Historically, the character for *sun* began as looking something like the sun but evolved into a box with a line through it. The average Chinese reader thinks no more of the origins of the character than the English reader thinks of the origins of *sun* in Old English or of the origins of the individual letters in Phoenician. There are sometimes clues to meaning or pronunciation in the parts that make up each character, however. Three lines on the left side of the character may indicate that the character has to do with liquid, for example. Chinese children begin school by learning the romanization system called *pinyin*, which helps them read as they acquire the characters. Japanese and Korean children begin to read using syllabic systems.

Syllabic writing systems have been found in a number of places. Sequoyah developed a syllabic system for the Cherokee language in the 19th century in the United States. Japanese makes use of two syllabic systems, collectively called *kana*. *Hiragana* is the first script taught in elementary school and is used among adults primarily to write grammatical endings. *Katakana* is used for non-Chinese foreign loan words and for emphasis, in the way English printing uses italics. There are, depending on how they are counted, almost 50 *hiragana* and 50 *katakana*. They represent vowels (*a, i, u, e, o*), consonant-vowel combinations (*ka, ki, ku, ke, ko,* etc.), and *n,* which can only be used by itself at the end of a word.

A special case of syllabic writing (Sampson [1985] calls the system "featural" rather than "syllabic") is *Han'gul,* the Korean script. *Han'gul* combines 10 basic vowels with 14 basic consonants into an ingenious system of syllable shapes. If the vowel of the syllable is written oriented along a vertical axis, it is placed to the right of the consonant. If the vowel is written oriented along the horizontal axis, the consonant goes above it. In a consonant-vowel-consonant grouping, the second consonant has a predictable place below the consonant and vowel combination. The result is a square grouping that reminds some people of simplified Chinese characters but is much quicker to learn.

The word *hotel* in nine languages. Left column: Arabic, Swahili, Chinese, Italian. Right column: Japanese, Hungarian, Hindi, Korean, Welsh.

Teaching Scenarios

1. Your colleague at an elementary school comments that her first grade students can't seem to come to the point during their "show and tell" time. What may be happening?
2. A university student from Kuwait is enrolled in a first-year composition class your friend is teaching. Your friend comments that the student's English grammar is good but that the essays the student produces seem disorganized. What information can you give your friend that might help her understand her student?

 Check Your Knowledge

1. What differences have been theorized between speech and writing? Can we say they are true?
2. How does the language of the Internet relate to speech and writing? Is it more like speech or more like writing?
3. What criticisms have been made of the distinction between orality and literacy?
4. What clashes may be found between home and school literacies?
5. What are some issues in bilingual literacy?
6. How may it be said that writing is socially constructed?
7. What is contrastive rhetoric, and what criticisms have been made of the research in it?
8. Be able to define these terms:

   genre
   discourse community
   syncretic literacy
   funds of knowledge
   contrastive rhetoric
   alphabetic script
   syllabic script
   logographic script

Apply Your Knowledge

1. What are the differences between schooled and unschooled literacies? When you acquire school literacy, what else do you acquire?
2. Have you tried to learn to read and write in another language? What were your experiences?

Reflect

What forms of literacy do you use daily? What things besides reading long texts and writing term papers might be considered literacy?

Expand Your Knowledge

1. Read *Ways with Words* (Heath 1983) and report on Heath's study. Find articles or books that make reference to her work.
2. Volunteer at a family literacy project. Teach someone how to read.
3. We have mentioned only a few representative scripts in this chapter. Find out about others, either contemporary or historical.
4. Find out more about contrastive rhetoric research.

Suggested Readings

David Barton. *Lietracy: An Introduction to the Ecology of Written Language*. Cambridge: Blackwell, 1994.

William Grabe and Robert B. Kaplan. *Theory and Practice of Writing: An Applied Linguistic Perspective*. London: Longman, 1996.

Appendix A
Languages of the World

What's the most commonly spoken language in the world?

According to the 2003 edition of Ethnologue *(www.sil.org/ethnologue)*, these were the top 20 languages, measured by the number of native speakers (numbers in millions):

1. Mandarin Chinese (885)
2. Spanish (332)
3. English (322)
4. Bengali (189)
5. Hindi (182)
6. Portuguese (170)
7. Russian (170)
8. Japanese (125)
9. German (98)
10. Chinese, Wu (77.2)
11. Javanese (75.5)
12. Korean (75)
13. French (72)
14. Vietnamese (67.7)
15. Telugu (66.4)
16. Chinese, Yue (66)
17. Arabic (64.9)
18. Marathi (64.8)
19. Tamil (63.1)
20. Turkish (59)

This list needs at least two comments. First, these are the numbers for native speakers. The list does not include people who have learned the languages as second or foreign languages. Getting those sorts of numbers is difficult, because such a process would involve having to assess how effective the second/foreign language learning was. That is, when is a person credited with speaking a language? Must that person be able to read and write in the language as well as speak it? Second, you will have noticed that *Chinese* appears three times, as Mandarin, Wu, and Yue. What we consider *Chinese* is really a complex of related varieties; Mandarin is considered the national language of China. Wu is the variety spoken around Shanghai. Yue is sometimes called Cantonese and is spoken in southern China.

How Are These Languages Distributed?

Ethnologue (2003) breaks down geographic distribution in this way:

	Total Living Languages	Percentage
The Americas	1,013	15%
Africa	2,058	30%
Europe	230	3%
Asia	2,197	32%
The Pacific	1,311	19%
Total	6,809	

The 6,809 languages in the world are grouped in approximately 100 families. We will first survey some of the world's largest language families.

Indo-European

The *Indo-European* family is made up of more than 400 languages spread across Europe and Asia. Included in Europe are Germanic (English, German, and Scandinavian languages); Italic (Latin and the Romance languages such as French, Spanish, Italian, Portuguese, and Romanian); Greek; Slavic (Polish, Russian, Ukranian, Czech, and Slovak); and Celtic (Welsh and Gaelic). In Asia, more than 300 *Indo-Iranian* languages are found in India, Pakistan, Bangladesh, Iran, and Afghanistan. They include Gujarati, Hindi, Urdu, Bengali, Marathi, Farsi/Persian, and Pashto.

African Language Families

Africa is home to four major language families. The first is the *Afro-Asiatic* family, which includes the Semitic languages (Arabic and Hebrew among them) as well as Berber, found in northern Africa. Chadic languages, the most important of which is Hausa, are spoken in Nigeria, Chad, and Cameroon. Cushitic languages are spoken in an area from Ethiopia and Somalia to Kenya and Tanzania. Omotic languages are spoken in Ethiopia.

Niger-Congo (sometimes called Niger-Kordofanian) languages are spoken across Africa, from Mali and Guinea-Bissau in the west to Kenya and Tanzania in the east and to South Africa and Botswana in the south. It is a very large family, with 1,489 languages. Swahili and Zulu are both in the Bantu group of Niger-Congo languages. Fulani and Wolof, important languages in western Africa, are not Bantu languages, but they are Niger-Congo languages.

The *Nilo-Saharan* family consists of about 200 languages spoken in central Africa. Among them are Masai, Luo, Dinka, and a number of Nubian languages.

The smallest major language family in Africa is *Khoisian*, with fewer than 30 languages, all spoken in southern Africa (South Africa, Botswana, Angola, and Namibia).

Languages of Asia and the Pacific

There are six major language families in the Asia/Pacific region. The largest group is the *Austronesian* family, which includes more than 1,200 languages spoken on islands in the Pacific Ocean from Taiwan and the Philippines through Indonesia and Papua New Guinea to Fiji and Samoa. The widest ranging members of the family are Maori (New Zealand) and Hawaiian. This family includes the national languages of the Philippines (Tagalog), Malaysia (Bahasa Malaysia), and Indonesia (Bahasa Indonesia) and the widely spoken language Javanese (Indonesia).

Sino-Tibetan languages include Chinese (14 varieties, by some counts) as well as the Karen languages spoken in Myanmar and Thailand and the Tibeto-Burman languages, which have spread across southeast Asia and southern China.

The *Austro-Asiatic* family consists of Vietnamese and Khmer and a number of other languages found across southeastern Asia from Vietnam through Cambodia and Laos to northeastern India.

Dravidian languages are spoken in central and southern India. They include Tamil and Telugu.

The *Altaic* family is found across central Asia from Turkey to Mongolia. There are about 40 languages in the Turkic sub-group, which includes Turkish, Azerbaijani, Kazakh, and Uzbek. Some linguists put Korean in the Altaic family, while others believe it a separate, isolate, language.

There are perhaps 100, often very endangered, languages in the *Australian* family. These are the indigenous languages of the continent. About 250 languages have been identified as belonging to this family, but most have become extinct.

The Americas

There are at least 59 families of indigenous languages in the Americas. Many of them are endangered. *Eskimo-Aleut* languages are spoken in an arc across the top of the world, from Greenland to Siberia through Canada and Alaska. Yupik is a group of western languages. Inuktikut is the language of the Inuit people.

The *Algic* family has as its major group the Algonquian languages, which include Cree, Ojibwa, Shawnee, Arapaho, and Cheyenne.

The *Na-Dene* family includes both Tlingit, spoken in Alaska, and Navajo, spoken in Arizona, New Mexico, and Utah. Navajo is the American Indian language with the largest number of speakers.

Siouan languages include Mandan, Dakota, Lakota, and Crow. They were the languages of the central plains of the United States and Canada.

The *Muskogean* family includes southern U.S. languages such as Alabama, Muskogee, Choctaw, and Chickasaw and northwestern ones like Salish and Coeur D'Alene.

Uto-Aztecan is a large, relatively robust family. It includes Hopi, Comanche, and Paiute in the United States and Nahuatl (Aztec), Mayan, and Quich'e in Mexico and Guatemala.

The *Quechuan* family consists of about 45 languages with about six million speakers in the Andean region of South America (primarily Peru, Ecuador, and Bolivia).

Isolates

Linguists have not been able to find families for some of the world's languages. They call these *isolates*. Among the most famous isolates are Basque, spoken in France and Spain; Japanese, one of the world's most spoken languages; Ainu, the indigenous language of Japan; and Zuni, a language of the U.S. southwest. As we have mentioned, Korean also may in fact be an isolate.

This survey excludes much, but it will serve for introductory purposes. We have not mentioned dozens of families, including most of those in Amazonia, Papua New Guinea, and Indonesia, all very linguistically fertile, though threatened, parts of the world.

Appendix B
How Languages Are Put Together

We offer Appendix B as a reference guide. We assume that students who are using this book have taken, or will take, a separate introduction to language/linguistics class for more detailed and technical descriptions. We recognize, however, that some teachers using this textbook would like to include a brief introduction to linguistic description in their course. We point out that our approach is descriptive rather than theoretical. We will use primarily English for our examples because we are confident the readers of this book know the language well.

The Sounds of Language

Phonetics is the study of sounds in languages. In this brief overview, we will confine ourselves to using an articulatory approach, which looks at how sounds are produced by the body. We will be using some of the symbols of the **International Phonetic Alphabet** (IPA) in this appendix. The IPA is a convention used by linguists to record speech without having to depend on the inconsistencies of spelling systems.

Fundamentally, English speech sounds are produced by forcing air from the lungs out through the oral or nasal cavities (the mouth and nose). As the air is forced up the trachea (windpipe), it encounters the larynx (voice box) at the top of the trachea. Inside the larynx are the vocal cords. You can feel them by covering your ears with your hands, making a long [s] sound and then changing the [s] to a [z] sound. When saying [s], you shouldn't feel a buzzing vibration. When you say [z], you should. When you say [s], the glottis, the opening between the vocal chords, is open, and with [z] it is vibrating. Sounds made with an open glottis are **voiceless;** sounds made with a vibrating glottis are **voiced.** The distinction between voiceless and voiced is seen in the English pairs [s]/[z], [p]/[b], [t]/[d], and [k]/[g], among others.

To describe English consonants, we need, in addition to information about voicing, to describe place and manner of articulation. The place of articulation is where the air is stopped or slowed. The following are **places of articulation,** with examples for each:

- *bilabial* (two lips): [p] and [m]
- *labiodental* (lower lip, upper teeth): [f] and [v]
- *interdental* (tip of tongue between front teeth): [θ] as in *th*igh and [ð] as in *th*y
- *alveolar* (tongue on or near the ridge behind the front teeth): [t] and [s]
- *palatal* (tongue near the hard palate): [š] in di*sh* and [tč] in rea*ch*
- *velar* (made with the soft palate): [k] and [g]
- *glottal* (with glottis): [h] and the sound in the middle of bu*tt*on

You may have noticed that some parts of the oral cavity are not used in English as places of articulation. The uvula (which hangs down in the back of the throat) is used as an articulator in Farsi and French. The pharynx (back of the throat) is used in Arabic.

The **manner of articulation** refers to how the air is stopped or slowed. In English, we have these processes:

- *stops* (air is stopped completely in the mouth): [p], [t], and [k]
- *fricatives* (air is almost completely stopped and a hissing is produced): [š] in *sh*ort and [f]
- *affricatives* (air is stopped and then released): [tč] in *ch*urch and [dz] in *j*udge
- *nasals* (the nasal passage is open and air flows through): [m] and [n]
- *liquids* (air is only partially blocked and escapes around tongue): [l] and [r]
- *glides* (very little obstruction at all): [w]

Again, English does not exhaust the possibilities of sounds that can be made in other languages. Consider the trill in Spanish, the "rolled" r in *perro*.

We combine descriptions of place and manner of articulation with voicing to describe consonants. Thus, [p] is a bilabial voiceless stop and [v] a labiodental voiced fricative.

Vowels are made with the airstream relatively unobstructed. They are described in a different way from consonants. First of all, vowels are almost always voiced. The following four processes are taken into account when describing vowels:

- Is the tongue raised or lowered? (high/mid/low vowels)

To feel tongue height, say *beat, bet, bat* or *rue, row, raw*. In either case, you are going from high vowels to mid to low.

- Is the tongue moving forward or backward? (front/mid/back vowels)

Now say *beat/but, lay/low,* and *feather/father*. You are moving from front vowels to back.

- Is the sound produced in a tense or relaxed way? (tense/lax vowels)

To feel the tense/lax contrast, say *beat/bit* and *date/debt*. Here, you are moving from tense to lax.

- Are the lips rounded or not? (rounded/unrounded vowels)

There are only four rounded vowels in English. To get an idea of rounding, say the sounds in *root, put, boat,* and *caught*.

Thus, the vowel in *beat* may be described as high, front, tense, and unrounded. While the only rounded vowels in English are also back vowels, this does not mean, of course, that there are no other possibilities. French and German both have rounded front vowels. Though all the vowels of English are made in the oral cavity, French and Portuguese have nasalized vowels.

Dipthongs are two-part vowel sounds made up of a vowel and a glide. Some dipthongs in English are [oy], as in *boy*, [ay] as in *buy*, and [aw] as in *now*.

We noted at the beginning that English uses air forced out of the lungs to make sound. Several southern African languages make use of click sounds, similar to the disapproving English *tsk tsk*, as consonants. These clicks may be made with many different places of articulation. Other African and some Native American languages make use of incoming (implosive) air in addition to outgoing (egressive) air.

So far, we have considered the segmental aspects of sound. Now we will look at the **suprasegmental** aspects, at units beyond individual sounds. In English, we are familiar with stress and intonation. **Stress** is found at the syllable level and is sometimes called accent. In a word, the loudest syllable, the one said with the most energy, is stressed. English stress is unpredictable, for the most part, and must be learned with each new word. Other languages have predictable stress. Czech stresses the first syllable of each word. Welsh stresses the next-to-last syllable. Stress also affects the rhythm of a language. In English sentences, stress tends to get distributed at regular intervals, broken up by unstressed syllables. Certain syllables may be drawn out for emphasis. The result is a "tum de dum" sound to English sentences. We say English is a stressed-timed language. French and Spanish, on the other hand, are syllable-timed languages. The sound of their sentences is more staccato because stressed syllables are produced at regular intervals *(tat tat tat)*.

Intonation refers to the rise and fall of sentences. In English, statements and wh- questions fall at the end. Yes/no questions rise. Choice questions (*Would you like coffee or tea?*) rise and then fall.

A number of languages rely on **tones** to differentiate meaning. The most famous example is probably the word *ma* in Mandarin Chinese. Said with a high level tone it means *mother*. With a high rising tone, it means *hemp*. A falling and then rising tone signals the meaning *horse*. *Ma* said with a high falling tone is the word *scold*. *La* with the high, level tone means *pull*, with a falling tone *spicy*. Of course, context within the sentence provides meaning. In written language, the Chinese character for each word is different, so the reader immediately understands.

The last unit of suprasegmental information we will consider is **length**. In English, lengthened sounds have no meaning. In Finnish, the word *muta* means *mud*. If you hold the sound of the first vowel longer, the meaning becomes *some other*. If you hold the [t] a little longer, the meaning becomes *but*. In Japanese, the words for *aunt* and *grandmother* differ in speech only in the lengthening of the second vowel (*oba/obaa*). In the Italian phrase *una rosa rossa* (a red rose), *rosa* (rose) sounds different from *rossa* (red, feminine). These lengthenings are almost impossible for a native speaker of English to hear because such a process has no meaning in our language.

Phonology is the study of how sounds are organized in languages. Every language divides sounds differently. For example, in English, we consider the [p] in *pit* to be the same sound as the [p] in *spit*, even though the former sound actually differs from the latter in that it is spoken with a puff of air. (Try it. Hold a small piece of paper or lit match in front of your mouth as you say the words). It is possible to conceive of an instance in which the aspiration (puff) of a [p] would make for a difference in meaning, however, and indeed this happens in Hindi. Whether or not a [p] is aspirated is as important to a Hindi speaker as the difference between [t] and [d] is to an English speaker (a *pot* is not a *pod*). A **phoneme** is the smallest unit of language that helps distinguish meaning. The various manifestations of the phoneme are called **allophones**. So, in English, aspirated and unaspirated [p] are allophones of the phoneme /p/. We may thus also define **phoneme** as the mental representation of a sound. In Hindi, aspirated and unaspirated [p] are phonemes, because the presence or absence of aspiration causes a difference in meaning. Similarly, the [l] sounds in *leaf* and *pool*, though they are clearly said differently, are considered allophones of the phoneme /l/ in English, while in Russian they are considered different phonemes.

Words and Their Parts

A **morpheme** is the smallest unit of language with a distinct meaning, for phonemes, though they contribute to meaning, have no meaning in themselves. Morphemes may or may not be the same thing as words. A morpheme is a unit of meaning that cannot be broken down any further. So *dog* is a morpheme, but so is the verb *put on* (*He put on his shirt*). *Put* and *on* need each other to have a particular meaning. *Dog* is a morpheme, but *dogs* is two morphemes, *dog* and *–s*, the plural marker in English.

Free morphemes (known as roots or stems) can appear alone: *dog, cat, president, fly*. **Bound morphemes** (affixes) must be attached to a root. Affixes are of three kinds:

- *prefixes* (before the root): *un-, super-, pre-*
- *suffixes* (after the root): *-ly, -s, -ed*
- *infixes* (in the middle): a-*whole*-nother, un-*freakin'*-believable.

English uses infixes for emphasis, but some languages use infixes to convey morphological information; for example, in Tagalog (Philippines), *um* is used as an infix in ways that English uses the suffix *–er*, in its sense of "someone who does something."

Morphemes can also be divided into **inflectional** and **derivational**. Inflectional morphemes mark grammatical categories like TENSE (walk*ed*), PLURALITY (girl*s*), and THIRD PERSON (He walk*s*). In English, they are suffixes only. Derivational morphemes change the meaning of a word or its part of speech. They may be either prefixes (*un-, pre-*) or suffixes (*-ly, -able*).

Languages may be classified according to the way they put morphemes together. There are two basic morphological types of language, analytical (isolating) languages and synthetic languages. Analytical languages use strings of free morphemes. Mandarin Chinese is an important example. The sentence *Wô shi mêiguó rén* means *I am an American* (literally *I am America person*). The sentence *Wô men shi mêiguó rén* means *We are Americans*. The notion of PLURALITY is conveyed not by a suffix, as in English, but by a separate free morpheme, *men*.

Synthetic languages allow bound morphemes to be attached to roots. Sometimes, as in the agglutinative languages, a number of morphemes, each having one separate meaning, will be combined. Swahili verb stems are combined with one prefix that indicates PERSON (I, you, etc.) and another prefix that signals TENSE, so *ni-na-soma (I read)* and *ni-li-soma (I read*, past tense). In fusional languages, the meaning of the bound morphemes is often fused together, so in Spanish the *–o* in *hablo (I speak)* conveys both the notion of present tense and that of first person singular; the two meanings cannot be separated.

Sentences

Morphemes are put together to create sentences. **Syntax** studies the orderliness of sentences. It is the subfield that has been at the heart of linguistics for decades. Because it is such a well-developed area of study, it presents a mine field for those trying to put together a short sketch of the possibilities of language organization. We have opted to ignore theory and focus completely on the possibilities of sentence organization across languages.

Sentences are composed of words ordered within phrases. Languages order their sentences in characteristic but limited ways. In English, for example, we know that

Kicked the happy boy the ball

is an ungrammatical sentence. (Linguists mark ungrammatical sentence with *). After some thought, we are able to say why we think so; in English, the subject (the happy boy) comes before the verb (kicked), which comes before the direct object (the ball), in shorthand S-V-O. We can say that English is an S-V-O language.

While some languages, notably Latin, have a relatively free word order, most have a "default" or **unmarked** sentence pattern. Other (**marked**) patterns may be found, for example in poetry or for emphasis (*Bob I saw—not Tom*), but one pattern remains basic.

It is not the S-V-O of English, though it is the pattern of approximately one-third of the world's languages, that is the most common in the world, but the S-O-V pattern, found in 44 percent of the world's languages, such as Japanese and Korean. The V-S-O pattern of Welsh and Arabic, among others, accounts for almost 20 percent of languages. A few languages, such as Malagasy, have a V-O-S pattern. Only recently have linguists described examples of object initial languages (O-S-V, O-V-S), all in the Amazon Basin.

In our example, *Kicked the happy boy the ball,* how did we know to move *the happy boy* and *the ball* as units to make the correct sentence *The happy boy kicked the ball*? Sentences are more than collections of single words. They are structured through groups of words called *constituents*. The sentence

Most university students take over four years to graduate

can be divided as

(Most university students) (take over four years to graduate)

or S-V
and further divided

(Most university students) (take) (over four years) (to graduate)

and so on, until we reach individual words. Note that we divide sentences into constituents depending on meaning. It would be possible in another context to group *over* not with *four years* but with *take* as in (*The students*) (*take over*) (*the beaches*) (*every Spring Break*).

Certain classes of words perform certain functions within sentences. The names of the following classes may remain familiar to you from high school:

- nouns
- verbs
- adjectives
- adverbs

Over is an adverb in the first previous example, part of a two-word verb in the second.

These four classes are all **open classes**. That is, the category "verb" can always be expanded by new words (*to fax, to gross out*). **Closed classes** (function words) such as

- determiners *(the, many, my)*
- auxiliary verbs *(can, should, do)*
- prepositions *(in, at, on)*
- conjunctions *(and, but, or)*
- pronouns *(I, me, it)*

remain closed because languages typically do not add new words to these categories.

Words can be expanded to phrases, and the phrase will play the same role in a sentence. Thus, a noun or noun phrase may both be the subject of a sentence:

- *Brian drove up in a car.*
- *Two students drove up in a car.*
- *My friend from Utah drove up in a car.*
- *The people that we met last week drove up in a car.*

Among other phrase types are verb phrases *(loves loud music)*, adjective phrases *(well educated)*, adverb phrases *(as well as could be expected)*, and prepositional *phrases (in the garden)*.

To return to the notion of word order, languages tend to be consistent in placing the *head* of a phrase (central word: noun in a noun phrase, etc.). Languages are classified as *head initial* or *head final*. English is head initial, Japanese head final, thus:

- (Tom) (read a book): Noun Phrase plus Verb Phrase, with the verb at the beginning of its phrase=
- (Taro ga) (hon o yonda): Noun Phrase plus Verb Phrase, with the verb at the end of its phrase. (Literally, Taro SUBJECT MARKER book OBJECT MARKER read)
- (Tom) (is) (in the garden): Noun Phrase plus Verb Phrase plus Prepositional Phrase, with the preposition at the beginning of its phrase=
- (Taro ga) (niwa ni) (iru): Noun Phrase plus Prepositional (actually, for obvious reasons, *Post*positional) Phrase plus Verb Phrase, with the postposition at the end of its phrase (Literally, Taro SUBJECT MARKER garden in is)

We will leave our description of sentence organization at this admittedly rudimentary level.

Appendix C
Resources

Appendix C provides information regarding journals, conferences/associations, and databases in the field. Each can be located using an Internet search. Due to the transient nature of websites, we have not included individual URLs here.

Journals in the Field

General

Annual Review of Anthropology
Annual Review of Applied Linguistics
Anthropological Linguistics
Anthropology and Education
Applied Linguistics
International Review of Applied Linguistics
Journal of Language Identity and Education
Journal of Linguistic Anthropology
Language
Linguistics
Linguistics and Education
Semiotica

Language and Interaction/Language Variation

Discourse and Society
Discourse Processes
Discourse Studies
Human Communication Research
International Journal of the Sociology of Language
Journal of Pragmatics

Journal of Social Psychology
Journal of Sociolinguistics
Language and Intercultural Communication
Language in Society
Multilingua
Pragmatics
Research on Language and Social Interaction
Signs: Journal of Women in Culture and Society
Text
Women and Language

Learning Language and Culture, First and Second

Canadian Modern Language Review
Child Development
Child Language
Developmental Psychology
The ELT Journal
Foreign Language Annals
International Journal of Bilingual Education and Bilingualism
International Journal of Bilingualism
Journal of Child Language
Language Learning
Language Teaching
Language Teaching Research
Modern Language Journal
Second Language Research
Studies in Second Language Acquisition
System
TESOL Quarterly

Language Contact

English Today Quarterly
Journal of Multilingual and Multicultural Development
World Englishes

Literacy

College Communication and Composition
English for Specific Purposes
Journal of Second Language Writing
Reading in a Foreign Language
Reading Research Quarterly
Written Communication

Conferences/Associations

The following is a list of conferences and associations that address issues central to this book. For more information, consult their websites.

AILA (International Association of Applied Linguistics)
American Association of Applied Linguistics (AAAL)
Annual Ethnography in Education Research Forum
Georgetown University Roundtable
International Pragmatics
Language, Interaction, and Culture
New Ways of Analyzing Variation (NWAV)
Symposium about Language and Society-Austin (SALSA)
Teachers of English to Speakers of Other Languages (TESOL): international, state, and local

Databases

The following list provides starting places for research:

Academic Search Premier
Center for Advanced Research on Language Acquisition (CARLA)
Center for Applied Linguistics (CAL)
Educational Resources Information Center (ERIC)
Ethnologue
Linguistics and Language Behavior Abstracts (LLBA)

Glossary

acculturation: the process of internalizing the rules and behavior of a culture

acrolect: the most prestigious variety of a dialect

allophone: every way a phoneme can be produced

assimilation: the adoption of another culture through choice or necessity

backchannel: a type of feedback during conversation by which one person indicates understanding, interest, boredom, or other reactions

basic color term: a set of terms describing basic hues. There are at most 11 basic color terms, and the number depends on the language

basilect: the least prestigious form of a dialect

bound morpheme: the smallest unit of a language that has meaning, incapable of standing on its own. An example is the /s/ morpheme used in English to indicate plurality

Bulge Theory: the notion that remarkable similarities are found in the ways speakers address strangers and intimates (as opposed to acquaintances)

calque: a special kind of borrowed word, in which the borrowed word or phrase is translated into the receiving language's literal equivalent. Example: German *Fern-sprecher* from English *telephone*

child-directed speech: simplified speech used by adults to children in order to provide comprehensible input for language acquisition. Also called caretaker/caregiver speech

closed class: a group of words in a given language that stays the same and is not added to. Example: in English, prepositions

code switching: the use of two languages within one conversation or discourse, often as a way of announcing one's identity

Communication Accommodation Theory: process by which a speaker changes his/her way of speaking based on the conversational partner

communicative competence: the ability of a speaker to use a language beyond grammatical ability and including pragmatic, discourse, and social competence

competence: a person's knowledge of the rules needed to produce sentences in a given language. Also called I-language or internal language

connotation: meaning associated with a particular word, beyond the word's literal meaning; the feeling that attaches to a given word

contextualization cue: signals, such as intonation or rate of speech, that indicate to the hearer how the message is to be understood

contrastive rhetoric: Kaplan's idea that cultures have their own ways of organizing information in writing

co-operative principle: Grice's formulation of a general set of rules that speakers implicitly follow in order to communicate effectively

corpus planning: type of language planning that focuses mainly on standardizing the grammar, spelling, and vocabulary of a language

creole: a pidgin that has become the native language of a group

Critical Period Hypothesis: the notion that a child has a certain time to acquire a first language with native speaker competence

decontextualized language: abstract language; language outside of a definite situation

deficit model: the idea that differences in language show differences in intellectual ability; that is, speakers of a nonstandard variety are deemed by this theory to lack intellectual skills

denotation: the meaning of a word (compare with connotation)

derivational morpheme: a morpheme that is used to create new words from old. Derivational morphemes change the meaning of a word. Example: *-er* (*run* to *runner*)

dialect: a variety of language, based on a social or geographical distinction

diffusion: change that comes about as a result of one culture borrowing from another

diglossia: a situation in which two language varieties co-exist and are used for different purposes

dipthong: two vowels in one syllable

discourse community: a group that shares rules for language use

elaborated code: Bernstein's term for a variety of language that requires its users to make meaning explicit. Often identified with middle-class speech

ethnocentrism: the belief that one's own culture is superior; an inability to be sympathetic to other cultures

face: the public image projected by a person

foreigner talk: simplified language used to address nonnative speakers of a language; usually includes a lower rate of speech; simplified syntax; and generalized, non-specific vocabulary

fossilization: the stabilization of incorrect forms in second language acquisition; these forms become part of the speaker's language

frame: a cluster of information about a particular word, phrase, or situation that we have stored in our knowledge

free morpheme: the smallest unit of meaning that can stand on its own with its own meaning. Examples: *car, president.* Also called a *root* or a *stem*

funds of knowledge: the sum of knowledge gained as the result of lived experience; cultural knowledge, contrasted with knowledge gained from formal education

genre: discourse forms that share a set of characteristics, both formal and content based

high-context message: Hall's term for a message that contains little information but instead relies on the interlocutors sharing assumptions

high rise terminal (HRT): a rising intonation on an utterance that is actually a statement

illocutionary act: an act performed by a speaker in uttering a sentence; the force the speaker intends to have by uttering the sentence. Example: a promise

implicative: implied meaning; implicitly (indirectly) communicated idea

inflectional morpheme: the smallest unit of language used to mark a grammatical category. It is required by grammatical rules, and its addition does not change the meaning of the word. Example: the *-est* in *tallest*, the third person singular *-s* in *She runs*

interlanguage (IL): the language used by second language learners; an intermediate form that differs from both native and target languages

innovation: cultural change brought about as a result of invention

International Phonetic Alphabet (IPA): A set of symbols that allows linguists to represent sounds in any language, independent of the spelling of those words

intonation: variation of pitch (highest or loudness) in a sentence or phrase

IRE/IRF sequence: a common discourse pattern in education, wherein the teacher initiates a topic, the student responds, and the teacher makes a follow-up move of evaluation or feedback

kinesics: the study of body motion, including gestures, posture, touching, facial expressions, and eye contact

language: a structured system of sounds, words, gestures, and so forth used for communication

L1: a first or native language

L2: a language learned/acquired after the native language

Language of Wider Communication (LWC): a language that allows for communication among groups that do not speak the same language. Also known as lingua franca

language revitalization: the increased use of a language in everyday situations, prompted by increased teaching of the language or by other language planning means

length: the duration of a sound, how long it takes to say it

lingua franca: a language that allows for communication among groups that do not speak the same language. Also known as a Language of Wider Communication (LWC)

locutionary act: the act of uttering a sentence

low-context message: Hall's term for a message that must be made explicit because the interlocutors do not share assumptions

manner of articulation: how a sound is produced, by stopping, slowing, or interrupting the air stream

marked: any occurrence of a linguistic feature that is unusual or infrequent

mesolect: a middle variety of a dialect, occupying the middle of a continuum from acrolect to basilect; the variety is often used in daily situations

metaphor: a figure of speech in which a term is transferred from a literal meaning to something else. Example: My love is a red rose

morpheme: the small unit of linguistic meaning. Morphemes are made from phonemes. While the phonemes themselves have no meaning, their combination in the morpheme does

negative face: the desire not to be imposed upon or inconvenienced

nonstandard language: a variety that is often stigmatized and regarded as inferior to the standard language only because it differs from that standard or because it is spoken by members of the society who are powerless

onomatopoeia: a word that sounds like what it means. Example: *buzz*

open class: a group of words that is theoretically unlimited and can always be added to. Example: in English, verbs

paralanguage: a system that conveys information about the message during speech by varying pitch, loudness, rate of speech, and so forth

performance: the process by which one's competence is put to use. Also called E-language or external language

perlocutionary act: the effect, intended or not, of a speech act

phoneme: the mental image of a sound, or the smallest distinctive unit of a language

phonetics: the study of how sounds are produced in language

phonology: the study of the organization of sounds

pidgin: a language resulting from contact between two other languages, often used for trading purposes or in times of war

place of articulation: where a sound is produced, where air is stopped or slowed. Examples: *lips, teeth*

positive face: the desire to be thought well of; to have one's self-image boosted

pragmatics: the study of language in context, dealing with how sentences relate to the world around them, to speakers, and listeners

prototype: the best example of a given category

proxemics: the study of how space is used to communicate

restricted code: Bernstein's term for the variety of language rooted in concrete, specific circumstances. Often identified with the working class

Sapir-Whorf Hypothesis: a theory that claims language and thinking are interdependent. The language you speak is said to strongly affect the way you look at the world. Also called the Linguistic Relativity Hypothesis

schema: abstract mental representations that we build up as a result of experience

script: the information, based on the speaker's prior knowledge, that is connected with the meaning of a word. The script for the word *restaurant* contains the information that it is a place, there are people there who serve you food, etc.

semantic feature: a unit of meaning into which a word can be broken. The meaning is then seen as the sum of its features. Example: a *boy* is [+male] and [-adult]

sequential bilingualism: acquisition of two languages, one after the other, in childhood

simultaneous bilingualism: acquisition of two languages at the same time in childhood

socialization: the process of internalizing the rules and behavior of a culture

speech act: an utterance seen as an action by a speaker; each speech act consists of three separate acts: locutionary, illocutionary, and perlocutionary acts

speech event: the context in which speech acts are uttered

standard language: a language that is perceived to be the best, most prestigious variety in a given area

status planning: the type of language planning concerned with attitudes toward varieties, including which varieties should be taught in schools

stress: emphasis on a particular syllable within speech

suprasegmental: the aspects of pronunciation of an utterance that are larger than a sound segment. Examples: stress and intonation

synchronous time: an orientation to do more than one task at a time

syncretic literacy: literacy that combines practices from more than one tradition

syntax: the way words are put together to form phrases and sentences

tone: one of several pitches in a given language that helps convey meaning. Mandarin Chinese has four tones, so that one syllable can be produced in four different ways and convey four different meanings

transfer: the use of features from a native language in a second, nonnative one

unmarked: a usual, expected, frequent linguistic feature

voiced: the vibrating of the vocal chords when uttering a sound

voiceless: when a sound is made without the vibration of the vocal chords

References

Abel, Theodora M., and Francis L. K. Hsu. "Some Aspects of Personality of Chinese as Revealed by the Rorschach Test." *Journal of Projective Techniques* 13 (1949): 285–301.

Ard, Josh, and Taco Homburg. "Verification of Language Transfer." In *Language Transfer in Language Learning*, eds. Susan K. Gass and Larry Selniker. Amsterdam: John Benjamins, 1992.

Austin, J. L. *How to Do Things with Words*. Cambridge, MA: Harvard University Press, 1962/1975.

Axtell, Roger E. *Gestures: The Do's and Taboos of Body Language around the World*. 2d ed. New York: John Wiley & Sons, 1998.

Bachman, Lyle F., and Adrian S. Palmer. *Language Testing in Practice*. Oxford: Oxford University Press, 1996.

Baker, Colin, and Sylvia Prys Jones, eds. *Encyclopedia of Bilingualism and Bilingual Education*. Clevedon, UK: Multilingual Matters, 1998.

Baker, Victoria J. "Literacy in Developing Societies: Native Language versus National Language Literacy." In *Literacy Development in a Multilingual Context: Cross-Cultural Perspectives*, eds. Aydin Yucesan Durgunoglu and Ludo Verhoeven, 21–35. Mahwah, NJ: Lawrence Erlbaum Associates, 1998.

Ballenger, Cynthia. *Teaching Other People's Children: Literacy and Learning in a Bilingual Classroom*. New York: Teachers College Press, 1999.

Bardovi-Harlig, Kathleen, and Beverly S. Hartford. "Learning the Rules of Academic Talk: A Longitudinal Study of Pragmatic Change." *Studies in Second Language Acquisition* 15 (1993): 279–304.

Bartlett, Frederic C. *Remembering: A Study in Experimental and Social Psychology*. Cambridge: Cambridge University Press, 1932.

Basso, Keith H. "The Ethnography of Writing." In *Explorations in the Ethnography of Speaking*, eds. Richard Bauman and Joel Sherzer, 415–32. Cambridge: Cambridge University Press, 1989.

———. *Western Apache Language and Culture: Essays in Linguistic Anthropology*. Tucson: University of Arizona Press, 1990.

Baugh, John. *Beyond Ebonics: Linguistic Pride and Racial Prejudice*. New York: Oxford University Press, 2000.

Bayley, Robert, and Sandra R. Schecter, eds. *Language Socialization in Bilingual and Multilingual Societies*. Clevedon, UK: Multilingual Matters, 2003.

Becker, A. L. *Beyond Translation: Essays toward a Modern Philology*. Ann Arbor: University of Michigan Press, 1995.

Beebe, Leslie M., Tomoko Takahashi, and Robin Uliss-Weltz. "Pragmatic Transfer in ESL Refusals." In *Developing Communicative Competence in a Second Language*, eds. Robin C. Scarcella, Elaine Anderson, and Stephen D. Krashen. New York: Newbury House, 1990.

Benton, Richard, and Nena Eslao Benton. "RLS in Aotearoa/New Zealand 1989–1999." In *Can Threatened Languages Be Saved? Reversing Language Shift, Revisited: A 21st Century Perspective*, ed. Joshua A. Fishman, 423–50. Clevedon, UK: Multilingual Matters, 2001.

Berlin, Brent, and Paul Kay. *Basic Color Terms: Their Universality and Evolution.* Berkeley: University of California Press, 1969.

Bernstein, Basil B. *Class, Codes and Control, Vol. 1: Theoretical Studies toward a Sociology of Language.* London: Routledge & Kegan Paul, 1971.

———. *Pedagogy, Social Control, and Identity: Theory, Research, Critique.* 2d ed. Lanham, MD: Rowman & Littlefield, 2000.

Biber, Douglas. *Variation across Speech and Writing.* Cambridge: Cambridge University Press, 1988.

Birdwhistell, Ray L. *Kinesics and Context: Essays on Body Motion Communication.* Philadelphia: University of Pennsylvania Press, 1970.

Blom, Jan-Petter, and John J. Gumperz. "Social Meaning in Linguistic Structure: Code-Switching in Norway." In *Directions in Sociolinguistics: The Ethnography of Communication,* eds. John J. Gumperz and Dell Hymes, 407–34. New York: Holt, Rinehart and Winston, 1972. Repr., Oxford: Basic Blackwell, 1986.

Boas, Franz. 1966. *Introduction to the Handbook of American Indian Languages.* 1911. Repr., Lincoln: University of Nebraska Press, 1966.

Bohannan, Laura. "Shakespeare in the Bush." *Natural History* 75 (1966): 28–33.

Bornstein, Marc H., Joseph Tal, Charles Rahn, Celia Z. Galperin, Marie-Germaine Pecheux, Martine Lamour, Sueko Toda, Hiroshi Azuma, Misako Ogino, and Catherine S. Tamis-LeMonda. "Functional Analysis of the Contents of Maternal Speech to Infants of Five and Thirteen Months in Four Cultures: Argentina, France, Japan, and the United States." *Developmental Psychology* 28 (1992): 1–10.

Bouton, Lawrence F. "A Cross-Cultural Study of the Ability to Interpret Implicatures in English." *World Englishes* 7, no. 2 (1988): 183–97.

———. "The Effective Use of Implicature of English: Why and How It Should Be Taught in the ESL Classroom." *Pragmatics and Language Learning Monograph* (1990): 43–52.

———. "The Interpretation of Implicatures in English by NNS: Does It Come Automatically—without Being Explicitly Taught?" *Pragmatics and Language Learning Monograph* 3 (1992): 65.

———. "Conversational Implicatual in a Second Language: Learned Slowly When Not Deliberately Taught." *Journal of Pragmatics* 22 (1994): 157–67.

Bowerman, Melissa, and Soonja Choi. "Shaping Meanings for Language: Universal and Language-Specific in the Acquisition of Spatial Semantic Categories." In *Language Acquisition and Conceptual Development,* eds. Melissa Bowerman and Stephen C. Levinson, 475–511. Cambridge: Cambridge University Press, 2001.

Boxer, Diana. *Complaining and Commiserating: A Speech Act View of Solidarity in Spoken American English.* New York: Peter Lang, 1993.

Boyson-Bardies, Benedicte de. *How Language Comes to Children: From Birth to Two Years.* Trans. M. B. DeBevoise. Cambridge: The MIT Press, 1999.

Boyson-Bardies, Benedicte de, L. Sagart, and C. Durand. "Discernable Differences in the Babbling of Infants according to Target Language." *Journal of Child Language* 11 (1984): 11–15.

Brantlinger, Ellen A. *The Politics of Social Class in Secondary School: Views of Affluent and Impoverished Youth.* New York: Teachers College Press, 1993.

———. "The Social Class Embeddedness of Middle School Students' Thinking about Teachers." *Theory into Practice* 33 (1994): 191–98.

Brown, Penelope, and Stephen C. Levinson. *Politeness: Some Universals in Language Usage.* Cambridge: Cambridge University Press, 1987.

Brown, Roger, and Albert Gilman. "The Pronouns of Power and Solidarity." In *Language and Social Context*, ed. Pier Paolo Giglioli, 252–82. Harmondsworth, UK: Penguin Books, 1972.

Canale, Michael. "On Some Dimensions of Language Proficiency." In *Issues in Language Testing Research*, ed. J. W. Oller, 333–42. Rowley, MA: Newbury House, 1983.

Canale, Michael, and Merrill Swain. "Theoretical Bases of Communicative Approaches to Second Language Teaching and Testing." *Applied Linguistics* 1 (1980): 1–47.

Candland, Douglas Keith. *Feral Children and Clever Animals: Reflections on Human Nature*. New York: Oxford University Press, 1993.

Carroll, John B. *Language, Thought and Reality: Selected Writings of Benjamin Lee Whorf*. Cambridge: The MIT Press, 1956.

Carson, Joan G. "Becoming Biliterate: First Language Influences." *Journal of Second Language Writing* 1 (1992): 37–60.

Carson, Joan G., and Gayle L. Nelson. "Chinese Students' Perceptions of ESL Peer Response Group Instruction." *Journal of Second Language Writing* 5 (1996): 1–19.

Cazden, Courtney B. *Classroom Discourse: The Language of Teaching and Learning*. 2d ed. Portsmouth, NH: Heinemann, 2001.

Chafel, Judith A. "Children's Views of Social Inequality: A Review of Research and Implications for Teaching." *The Educational Forum* 61 (1996): 46–57.

Chiu, Lian-Hwang. "A Cross-Cultural Comparison of Cognitive Styles in Chinese and American Children." *International Journal of Psychology* 7 (1972): 235–42.

Civan, Michele Burtoff. *The Haitians: Their History and Culture*. Washington, DC: Refugee Service Center of the Center for Applied Linguistics, 1994.

Clancy, Patricia M. "The Acquisition of Communicative Style in Japanese." In *Language Socialization across Cultures*, eds. Bambi B. Schieffelin and Elinor Ochs. Cambridge: Cambridge University Press, 1986.

Coates, Jennifer. *Women, Men and Language*. London: Longman, 1993.

Cohen, Andrew D. "Developing the Ability to Perform Speech Acts." *Studies in Second Language Acquisition* 18 (1996): 253–67.

Cohen, Andrew D., and Elite Olshtain. "The Production of Speech Acts by EFL Learners." *TESOL Quarterly* 27 (1993): 33–56.

Connor, Ulla, and Ann M. Johns. *Contrastive Rhetoric: Cross-Cultural Aspects of Second-Language Writing*. Cambridge: Cambridge University Press, 1996.

Crystal, David. *The Cambridge Encyclopedia of Language*. 2d ed. Cambridge: Cambridge University Press, 1997.

———. *Language and the Internet*. Cambridge: Cambridge University Press, 2001.

Cummins, Jim. *Empowering Minority Students*. Sacramento: California Association for Bilingual Education, 1989.

Curtiss, Susan. 1977. *Genie: A Psycholinguistic Study of a Modern-Day "Wild Child."* New York: Academic Press, 1977.

Delpit, Lisa D. "The Silenced Dialogue: Power and Pedagogy in Educating Other People's Children." *Harvard Educational Review* 58 (1988): 280–91.

Denison, Norman. "Some Observations on Language Variety and Plurilingualism." In *Sociolinguistics*, eds. J. B. Pride and J. Holmes. Harmondworth, UK: Penguin, 1972.

Duranti, Alessandro, and Elinor Ochs. *Syncretic Literacy: Multiculturalism in Samoan American Families*. Santa Cruz, CA: National Center for Research on Cultural Diversity and Second Language Learning, 1966.

Eble, Connie. *Slang and Sociability: In-Group Language among College Students*. Chapel Hill, NC: University of North Carolina Press, 1996.

Eckert, Penelope. *Jocks and Burnouts: Social Categories and Identity in the High School.* New York: Teachers College Press, 1989.

Eckman, Paul, ed. *Emotion in the Human Face.* 2d ed. Cambridge: Cambridge University Press, 1982.

Erickson, Frederick, and Jeffrey Schultz. *The Counselor as Gatekeeper: Social Interaction in Interviews.* New York: Academic Press, 1982.

Espinosa, Linda M. *Hispanic Parental Involvement in Early Childhood Programs.* Washington, DC: ERIC Clearinghouse on Elementary and Early Childhood Education, 1995.

Ess, Charles, with Fay Sudweeks, eds. *Culture, Technology, Communication: Towards an Intercultural Global Village.* Albany: State University of New York Press, 2001.

Fawcett, Edmund, Peter Ayrton, and Joan White, trans. *Lucien Malson, Wolf Children and the Problem of Human Nature and Jean Itard, the Wild Boy of Aveyron.* New York: Monthly Review Press, 1972.

Faul, S. *Guía del Tipico Norte Americano.* Barcelona: Ediciones de Bolsillo S.A., 1999.

Ferguson, Charles A. "Diglossia." *Word* 15 (1959): 325–40.

Fishman, Joshua A. "Bilingualism and Biculturalism as Individual and as Societal Phenomena." *Journal of Multilingual and Multicultural Development* 1 (1980): 1–15.

FitzGerald, Frances. *Fire in the Lake: The Vietnamese and the Americans in Vietnam.* Boston: Little, Brown and Company, 1972.

Flor, Alicia Martínez, Esther Uśo Juan, and Ana Fernandez Guerra, eds. *Pragmatic Competence and Foreign Languag Teaching.* Castelló: Universitat Jaume, 2003.

Freire, Paulo. *Pedagogy of the Oppressed.* Trans. M. B. Ramos. Rev. org. 1970 ed. New York: Continuum, 2000.

Gal, Susan. "Peasant Men Can't Get Wives: Language Change and Sex Roles in a Bilingual Community." *Language in Society* 7 (1978): 1–16.

Gass, Susan M., and Larry Selinker. *Second Language Acquisition: An Introductory Course.* 2d ed. Mahwah, NJ: Lawrence Erlbaum Associates, 2001.

Gass, Susan M., and Evangelina Varonis. "Incorporated Repairs in NNS Discourse." In *Variation and Second Language Acquisition,* ed. M. Eisenstein, 71–86. New York: Plenum, 1989.

Gee, James Paul. *Social Linguistics and Literacies: Ideologies in Discourses.* 2d ed. London: Taylor & Francis, 1996.

Geertz, Clifford. *The Interpretation of Cultures.* New York: Basic Books, 1973.

Genesee, Fred. *Program Alternatives for Linguistically Challenged Students.* Santa Cruz, CA: Center for Research on Education, Diversity and Excellence, 1999.

Gentner, Dedre, and Susan Golden-Meadows, eds. *Language in Mind: Advances in the Study of Language and Thought.* Cambridge: MIT Press, 2003.

Gibson, Margaret A. "Minorities and Schooling: Some Implications." In *Minority Status and Schooling: A Comparative Study of Immigrant and Involuntary Minorities,* eds. Margaret A. Gibson and John U. Ogbu, 357–81. New York: Garland, 1991.

Gibson, Margaret A., and John U. Ogbu, eds. *Minority Status and Schooling: A Comparative Study of Immigrant and Involuntary Minorities.* New York: Garland, 1991.

Giles, Howard, and Peter F. Powesland. *Speech Style and Social Evaluation.* New York: Academic Press, 1975.

Goodenough, Ward. "Cultural Anthropology and Linguistics." In *Language in Culture and Society: A Reader in Linguistics and Anthropology,* ed. Dell Hymes, 36–39. New York: Harper and Row, 1964.

Grabe, William, and Robert B. Kaplan. *Theory and Practice of Writing: An Applied Linguistic Perspective.* London: Longman, 1996.

Gregory, Eve, and Ann Williams. *City Literacies: Learning to Read across Generations and Cultures.* London: Routledge, 2000.

Grice, Herbert Paul. "Logic and Conversation." In *Syntax and Semantics 3: Speech Acts*, eds. Peter Cole and Jerry L. Morgan, 41–58. New York: Academic Press, 1975.

Groce, Nora Ellen. *Everyone Here Spoke Sign Language: Hereditary Deafness on Martha's Vineyard.* Cambridge, MA: Harvard University Press, 1985.

Gumperz, John J. "Discourse Strategies." In *Studies in Interactional Linguistics 1.* Cambridge: Cambridge University Press, 1982.

Gumperz, John J., and Steven C. Levinson. "Rethinking Linguistic Relativity." *Current Anthropology* 32 (1996): 613–23.

Hall, Edward T. *The Hidden Dimension.* New York: Doubleday, 1966.

———. *Beyond Culture.* New York: Doubleday, 1976.

Hampden-Turner, Charles M., and Fons Trompenaars. *Building Cross-Cultural Competence: How to Create Wealth from Conflicting Values.* New Haven: Yale University Press, 2000.

Heath, Shirley Brice. *Ways with Words: Language, Life and Work in Communities and Classrooms.* New York: Cambridge University Press, 1983.

Hinds, John. "Reader versus Writer Responsibility." In *Writing across Languages: Analysis of L2 Text*, eds. Ulla Connor and Robert B. Kaplan. Reading, MA: Addison-Wesley, 1987.

———. "Inductive, Deductive, and Quasi-Inductive: Expository Writing in Japanese, Korean, Chinese, and Thai." In *Coherence in Writing: Research and Pedagogical Perspectives*, eds. Ula Connor and Ann M. Johns, 89–109. Alexandria, VA: Teachers of English to Speakers of Other Languages, 1990.

Holmes, Janet. "Women's and Men's Apologies: Reflectors of Cultural Values." *Applied Linguistics* 10 (1989): 194–213.

Hongladarom, Soraj. "Global Culture, Local Cultures, and the Internet: The Thai Example." In *Culture, Technology, Communication: Towards an Intercultural Global Village*, eds. Charles Ess with Fay Sudweeks, 307–24. Albany: State University of New York Press, 2001.

Hymes, Dell. "Models of the Interaction of Language and Social Life." In *Directions in Sociolinguistics: The Ethnography of Communication*, eds. John J. Gumperz and Dell Hymes, 35–71. New York: Holt, Rinehart and Winston, 1972. Repr., Oxford: Basil Blackwell, 1986.

———. *Foundations in Sociolinguistics: An Ethnographic Approach.* Philadelphia: University of Pennsylvania Press, 1974.

Kachru, Braj B., ed. *The Other Tongue: English across Cultures.* 2d ed. Urbana: University of Illinois Press, 1992.

Kachru, Yamuna. "Culture, Context, and Writing." In *Culture in Second Language Teaching and Learning*, ed. Eli Hinkel, 75–89. Cambridge: Cambridge University Press, 1999.

Kaplan, Robert B. "Cultural Thought Patterns in Inter-Cultural Education." *Language Learning* 16 (1966): 1–20.

———. "Cultural Thought Patterns Revisited." In *Writing across Languages: Analysis of L2 Text*, eds. Ulla Connor and Robert B. Kaplan, 9–21. Reading, MA: Addision-Wesley, 1987.

Kay, Paul, and Luisa Maffi. "Color Appearance and the Emergence and Evolution of Basic Color Lexicons." *American Anthropologist* 101 (2000): 743–60.

Kendon, Adam. "Gesture." *Annual Review of Anthropology* 26 (1997): 109–28.

Kirkpatrick, Andy. "Traditional Text Structures and Their Influence on the Writing in Chinese and English of Contemporary Mainland Chinese Speakers." *Journal of Second Language Writing* 6 (1997): 223–44.

Krashen, Stephen, and Tracy Terrell. *The Natural Approach: Language Acquisition in the Classroom.* Rev. ed. Englewood Cliffs, NJ: 1996.

Kress, Gunther. *Literacy in the New Media Age*. London: Routledge, 2003.

Labov, William. *Language in the Inner City: Studies in the Black English Vernacular*. Philadelphia: University of Pennsylvania Press, 1969/1972.

Lakoff, George, and Mark Johnson. *Metaphors We Live By*. Chicago: University of Chicago Press, 1980.

Lakoff, Robin. *Language and Women's Place*. New York: Harper & Row, 1975.

Landau, Jabob M., and Barbara Kellner-Heinkele. *Politics of Language in the Ex-Soviet Muslim States*. Ann Arbor: University of Michigan Press, 2001.

Lave, Jean, and Etienne Wenger. *Situated Learning: Legitimate Peripheral Participation*. Cambridge, Cambridge University Press, 1991.

Lee, Tiffany, and Daniel McLaughlin. "Reversing Navajo Language Shift, Revisited." In *Can Threatened Languages Be Saved? Reversing Language Shift, Revisited: A 21st Century Perspective*, ed. J. A. Fishman, 23–43. Clevedon, UK: Multilingual Matters, 2001.

LePage, R. B., Pauline Christie, Baudouin Jurdant, A. J. Weekes, and Andree Tabouret-Keller. "Further Report on the Sociolinguistic Survey of Multilingual Communities: Survey of Cayo District, British Honduras." *Language in Society* 3 (1974): 1–32.

Levinson, Stephen C. "Language and Cognition: The Cognitive Consequences of Spatial Description in Guugu Yimithirr." *Journal of Linguistic Anthropology* 7 (1997): 98–131.

Levinson, Stephen C., Sotaro Kita, Daniel B. M. Haun, and Bjorn H. Rasch. "Returning the Tables: Language Affects Spatial Reasoning." *Cognition* 84 (2002): 155–88.

Li, Peggy, and Lila Gleitman. "Turning the Tables: Language and Spatial Reasoning. *Cognition* 83 (2002): 265–94.

Liebman, JoAnne D. "Toward a New Contrastive Rhetoric: Differences between Arabic and Japanese Rhetorical Instruction." *Journal of Second Language Writing* 1 (1992): 141–65.

Lobner, Sebastian. *Understanding Semantics*. New York: Oxford University Press, 2002.

Long, Michael. "The Role of the Linguistic Environment in Second Language Acquisition." In *Handbook of Second Language Acquisition*, eds. William C. Ritchie and Tej K. Bhatia, 413–68. San Diego, CA: Academic Press, 1996.

Losey, Kay M. *Listen to the Silences: Mexican American Interaction in the Composition Classroom and Community*. Norwood, NJ: Ablex, 1997.

Lucas, Ceil, Robert Bayley, Clayton Valli, Mary Rose, and Alyssa Wulf. "Sociolinguistic Variation." In *The Sociolinguistics of Sign Languages*, ed. Ceil Lucas. Cambridge: Cambridge University Press, 2001.

Lucy, John A. *Grammatical Categories and Cognition: A Case Study of the Linguistic Relativity Hypothesis*. New York: Cambridge University Press, 1992.

———. *Language Diversity and Thought: A Reformulation of the Linguistic Relativity Hypothesis*. Cambridge: Cambridge University Press, 1992.

Luria, A. R. *Cognitive Development: Its Cultural and Social Foundations*. Ed. Michael Cole. Trans. Martin Lopez-Morillas and Lynn Solotaroff. Cambridge, MA: Harvard University Press, 1976.

Lutz, Catherine. *Unnatural Emotions: Everyday Sentiments on a Micronesian Atoll and Their Challenge to Western Theory*. Chicago: University of Chicago Press, 1988.

Maltz, Daniel N., and Ruth A. Borker. "A Cultural Approach to Male-Female Miscommunication." In *Language and Social Identity*, ed. John J. Gumperz, 195–216. Cambridge: Cambridge University Press, 1982.

Mandelbaum, David, ed. *Selected Writings of Edward Sapir in Language, Culture, and Personality*. Berkeley: University of California Press, 1949.

Martin, Laura. "Eskimo Words for Snow: A Case Study in the Genesis and Decay of an Anthropological Example." *American Anthropologist* 88 (1986): 418–23.

Matsuda, Paul Kei. "Contrastive Rhetoric in Context: A Dynamic Model of L2 Writing." *Journal of Second Language Writing* 6 (1997): 45–60.

McNall, Miles, Timothy Dunnigan, and Jeylan T. Mortimer. "The Educational Achievement of the St. Paul Hmong." *Anthropology and Education Quarterly* 25 (1994): 44–65.

McNeill, David. *Hand and Mind: What Gestures Reveal about Thought.* Chicago: University of Chicago Press, 1992.

Metzger, Melanie, and Ben Bahan. "Discourse Analysis." In *The Sociolinguistics of Sign Languages*, ed. Ceil Lucas. Cambridge: Cambridge University Press, 2001.

Milroy, Leslie. *Language and Social Networks.* 2d ed. Oxford: Blackwell, 1987.

Mitchell-Kernan, Claudia. "Signifying and Marking: Two Afro-American Speech Acts." In *Directions in Sociolinguistics: The Ethnography of Communication*, eds. John J. Gumperz and Dell Hymes, 161–79. New York: Holt, Rinehart and Winston, 1972. Repr., Oxford: Basil Blackwell, 1986.

Moll, Luis, and Norma Gonzalez. "Lessons from Research with Language-Minority Children." *Journal of Reading Behavior* 26 (1994): 439–56.

Morgan, Marcyliena. *Language, Discourse and Power in African American Culture.* New York: Cambridge University Press, 2002.

Morikawa, H., N. Shand, and Y. Kosawa. "Maternal Speech to Prelingual Infants in Japan and the United States: Relationships among Functions, Forms, and Referents." *Journal of Child Language* 15 (1988): 237–56.

Morris, Michael W., Richard E. Nisbett, and Kaiping Peng. "Culture and Cause: American and Chinese Attributions for Social and Physical Events." *Journal of Personality and Social Psychology* 67 (1994): 949–71.

Morris, Michael W., Richard E. Nisbett, and Kaiping Peng. "Causal Attribution across Domains and Cultures." In *Causal Cognition*, eds. Dan Sperber, David Premack, and Ann James, 577–612. Oxford: Clarendon Press, 1995.

Nassaji, Hossein, and Gordon Wells. "What's the Use of 'Triadic Dialogue'?: An Investigation of Teacher-Student Interaction." *Applied Linguistics* 21 (2000): 376–406.

Neill, Sean. *Classroom Nonverbal Communication.* London: Routledge, 1991.

Nelms, Jodi. "The Role of Sarcasm in NS-NNS (Mis)Communication." Paper read at colloquium at the American Association for Applied Linguistics conference, Salt Lake City, Utah, 2002.

Ninio, Anat, and Catherine E. Snow. *Pragmatic Development.* Boulder: Westview Press, 1996.

Nisbett, Richard E. *The Geography of Thought: How Asians and Westerners Think Differently . . . and Why.* New York: The Free Press, 2003.

Nisbett, Richard E., Kaiping Peng, Incheol Choi, and Ara Norenzayan. "Culture and Systems of Thought: Holistic versus Analytic Cognition." *Psychological Review* 108 (2001): 291–310.

Ochs, Elinor. *Culture and Language Development: Language Acquisition and Language Socialization in a Samoan Village.* Cambridge: Cambridge University Press, 1988.

Olshtain, Elite, and Andrew D. Cohen. "The Learning of Complex Speech Act Behavior." *TESL Canada Journal* 7 (1990): 45–65.

Ong, Walter J. *Orality and Literacy: The Technology of the Word.* London: Routledge, 1982.

Onikawa, Denise L., Ormond W. Hammond, and Stan Koki. *Family Involvement in Education: A Synthesis of Research for Pacific Education.* Honolulu, HI: Pacific Resources for Education and Learning, 1998.

Osborne, A. Barry. "Practice into Theory into Practice: Culturally Relevant Pedagogy for Students We Have Marginalized and Normalized." *Anthropology and Education Quarterly* 27 (1996): 285–314.

Padden, Carol, and Tom Humphries. *Deaf in America: Voices from a Culture*. Cambridge, MA: Harvard University Press, 1988.

Padron, Yolanda N., Hersh C. Waxman, and Hector H. Rivera. *Educating Hispanic Students: Obstacles and Avenues to Improved Academic Achievement*. Santa Cruz, CA: Center for Research on Education, Diversity & Excellence, 2002.

Park, Stephen. *Class Politics: The Movement for the Students' Right to Their Own Language*. Urbana, IL: National Council of Teachers of English, 2000.

Paulston, Christina Bratt. "Pronouns of Address in Swedish: Social Class Semantics and a Changing System." *Language in Society* 5 (1976): 359–86.

———. *Linguistic Minorities in Multilingual Settings*. Philadelphia: John Benjamin, 1994.

Pavlenko, Aneta. "How Am I to Become a Woman in an American Vein?: Transformations of Gender Performance in Second Language Learning." In *Multilingualism, Second Language Learning, and Gender,* eds. Aneta Pavlenko, Adrian Blackledge, Ingrid Piller, and Marya Teustsch-Dwyer, 133–74. Berlin: Mouton de Gruyter, 2001.

Pavlenko, Aneta, Adrian Blackledge, Ingrid Piller, and Marya Teutsch-Dwyer. *Multilingualism, Second Language Learning, and Gender.* Berlin: Mouton de Gruyter, 2001.

Pederson, Eric. "Language as Context, Language as Means: Spatial Cognition and Habitual Language Use." *Cognitive Linguistics* 6 (1995): 33–62.

Pederson, Eric, Eve Danziger, David Wilkins, Stephen Levinson, Sotoro Kita, and Gunter Senft. "Semantic Typology and Spatial Conceptualization." *Language* 74 (1998): 557–89.

Perry, Theresa, and Lisa Delpit, eds. *The Real Ebonics Debate: Power, Language and the Education of African-American Children*. Boston: Beacon Press, 1998.

Peyton, Joy Kreeft, Donald A. Ranard, and Scott McGinnis. *Heritage Languages in America: Preserving a National Resource*. McHenry, IL: Delta Systems and Center for Applied Linguistics, 2001.

Philips, Susan Urmston. *Invisible Culture: Communication in Classroom and Community on the Warm Springs Indian Reservation*. Prospect Heights, IN: Waveland Press, 1983.

Poplack, Shana. "Sometimes I'll Start a Sentence in Spanish *y Termino en Español*." *Linguistics* 18 (1979/1980): 581–618.

Pullum, Geoffrey K. *The Great Eskimo Vocabulary Hoax and Other Irreverent Essays on the Study of Language*. Chicago: University of Chicago Press, 1991.

Purcell-Gates, Victoria. "Family Literacy." In *Handbook of Reading Research, Vol. 3*, eds. Michael Kamil, Peter B. Mosenthal, P. David Pearson, and Rebecca Barr, 853–70. Mahwah, NJ: Lawrence Erlbaum Associates, 2000.

Purves, Alan, and Gail Hawisher. "Writers, Judges, and Text Models." In *Developing Discourse Practices in Adolescence and Adulthood*, eds. Richard Beach and Susan Hynds, 183–99. Norwood, NJ: Ablex, 1990.

Radford, Andrew. *Syntax: A Minimalist Introduction*. Cambridge: Cambridge University Press, 1997.

Rickford, John R. *African American Vernacular English: Features, Evolution, Educational Implications*. Malden, MA: Blackwell, 1999.

Rogoff, Barbara. *The Cultural Nature of Human Development*. Oxford: Oxford University Press, 2003.

Rosch, Eleanor H. "On the Internal Structure of Perceptual and Semantic Categories." In *Cognitive Development and the Acquisition of Language*, ed. Timothy E. Moore, 111–44. New York: Academic Press, 1973.

Rose, Kenneth R. "Pragmatic Consciousness-Raising in an EFL Context." *Pragmatics and Language Learning Monograph Series* 5 (1994): 52–63.

Rose, Kenneth R., and Gabriele Kasper. *Pragmatics in Language Teaching.* New York: Cambridge University Press, 2002.

Sacks, Oliver. *Seeing Voices.* Berkeley: University of California Press, 1989.

Sampson, Geoffrey. 1985. *Writing Systems: A Linguistic Introduction.* Stanford: Stanford University Press, 1985.

Saussure, Ferdinand de. *Course in General Linguistics.* Eds. Charles Bally and Albert Reidlinger. Trans. W. Baskin. New York: McGraw-Hill, 1915/1959.

Savage-Rumbaugh, Sue, Stuart G. Shanker, and Talbot J. Taylor. *Apes, Language, and the Human Mind.* New York: Oxford University Press, 1998.

Schecter, Sandra R., and Robert Bayley. *Language as Cultural Practice: Mexicanos en el Norte.* Mahwah, NJ: Lawrence Erlbaum Associates, 2002.

Schieffelin, Bambi B. "Getting It Together: An Enthographic Approach to the Study of the Development of Communicative Competence." In *Developmental Pragmatics*, eds. Elinor Ochs and Bambi B. Schieffelin, 73–108. New York: Academic Press, 1979.

Schieffelin, Bambi B., and Elinor Ochs, eds. *Language Socialization across Cultures.* Cambridge: Cambridge University Press, 1986.

Schieffelin, Edward L. "Anger, Grief, and Shame: Toward a Kaluli Enthnopsychology." In *Person, Self, and Experience: Exploring Pacific Ethnopsychologies*, eds. Geoffrey M. White and John Kirkpatrick, 168–82. Berkeley: University of California Press, 1985.

Scollon, Ron, and Suzanne B. K. Scollon. *Narrative, Literacy, and Face in Interethnic Communication.* Norwood, NJ: Ablex, 1981.

Scollon, Ron, and Suzanne Wong Scollon. *Intercultural Communication: A Discourse Approach.* 2d ed. Oxford: Basil Blackwell, 2001.

Scribner, Sylvia, and Michael Cole. *The Psychology of Literacy.* Cambridge, MA: Harvard University Press, 1981.

Searle, John R. *Speech Acts.* Cambridge: Cambridge University Press, 1969.

Slobin, Dan I. "Two Ways to Travel: Verbs of Motion in English and Spanish." In *Grammatical Constructions: Their Form and Meaning*, eds. Masayoshi Shibatani and Sandra A. Thompson, 195–219. Oxford: Clarendon Press, 1996.

Smitherman, Geneva. *Talkin and Testifyin: The Language of Black America.* Detroit: Wayne State University Press, 1986.

Solomon, Jeff, and Nancy Rhodes. *Conceptualizing Academic Language.* Research Report Number 15. Santa Cruz, CA: National Center for Research on Cultural Diversity and Second Language Learning, 1995.

Spradley, J. *The Ethnographic Interview.* New York: Holt, Reinhart and Winston, 1979.

Steffeson, Margaret S., Chitra Joad-Dev, and Richard Anderson. "A Cross-Cultural Perspective on Reading Comprehension." *Reading Research Quarterly* 15 (1979): 10–29.

Street, Brian V. *Social Literacies: Critical Approaches to Literacy in Development, Ethnography and Education.* London: Longman, 1995.

Sunderland, Jane. "Issues of Language and Gender in Second and Foreign Language Education." *Language Teaching* 33 (2000a): 203–23.

———. "New Understandings of Gender and Language Classroom Research: Texts, Teacher Talk and Student Talk." *Language Teaching Research* 4 (2000b): 149–73.

Swain, M. "Communicative Competence: Some Roles of Comprehensible Input and Comprehensible Output in Its Development." *Input in Second Language Acquisition*, ed. Carolyn Madden, 235–53. Rowley, MA: Newbury House, 1985.

Swales, John. *Genre Analysis.* Cambridge: Cambridge University Press. 1990.

Swan, Joan. *Girls, Boys, and Language.* Oxford: Basil Blackwell, 1992.

Tannen, Deborah. *You Just Don't Understand*. New York: Ballantine Books, 1990.

Taylor, Insup. "Learning to Read in Chinese, Korean, and Japanese." In *Literacy Development in a Multilingual Context: Cross-Cultural Perspectives*, eds. Aydin Yucesan Durgunoglu and Ludo Verhoeven, 225–48. Mahwah, NJ: Lawrence Erlbaum Associates, 1998.

Tharp, Roland G., and Roland Gallimore. *Rousing Minds to Life: Teaching, Learning, and Schooling in Social Context*. Cambridge: Cambridge University Press, 1988.

Tharp, Roland G., and Lois A. Yamauchi. *Effective Instructional Conversation in Native American Classrooms*. Educational Practice Report Number 10. Santa Cruz, CA: National Center for Research on Cultural Diversity and Second Language Learning, 1994.

Thomason, Sarah G. *Language Contact: An Introduction*. Washington, DC: Georgetown University Press, 2001.

Tobin, Joseph J., David Y. H. Wu, and Dana H. Davidson. *Preschool in Three Cultures: Japan, China, and the United States*. New Haven, CT: Yale University Press, 1979.

Todd, Loreto. 1990. *Pidgins and Creoles*. 2d ed. London: Routledge, 1990.

Tomasello, Michael. *The Cultural Origins of Human Cognition*. Cambridge, MA: Harvard University Press, 1999.

Tonnies, Ferdinand. *Community and Society: Gemeinschaft and Gesselschaft*. Trans. and ed. Charles P. Loomis. New York: Harper & Row, 1957.

Tylor, Edward. *Primitive Culture: Researches into the Development of Mythology, Philosophy, Religion, Art, and Custom*. London: John Murray, 1871.

U.S. Department of Education, National Center for Educational Statistics. *The Condition of Education 2003*. NCES 2003-067. Washington, DC: U.S. Government Printing Office, 2003.

Varonis, Evangeline Marlos, and Susan M. Gass. "Miscommunication in Native/Non-Native Conversation." *Language in Society* 14 (1982): 114–36.

Villegas, Anna Maria, and Tamara Lucas. *Educating Culturally Responsive Teachers: A Coherent Approach*. Albany: State University of New York Press, 2002.

Vygotsky, L. S. *Mind in Society: The Development of Higher Psychological Processes*. Cambridge, MA: Harvard University Press, 1978.

Wagner, Daniel A. *Literacy, Culture, and Development: Becoming Literate in Morocco*. Cambridge: Cambridge University Press, 1993.

Wallace, Anthony F. C. *Culture and Personality*. New York: Random House, 1961.

Wallman, Joel. 1992. *Aping Language*. Cambridge: Cambridge University Press, 1992.

Werker, Janet F., and R. C. Tees. "Cross-Language Speech Perception: Evidence for Perceptual Reorganization during the First Year of Life." *Infant Behavior and Development* 7 (1984): 49–63.

Wolfson, Nessa A. "The Bulge: A Theory of Speech Behavior and Social Distance." In *Second Language Discourse: A Textbook of Current Research*, ed. J. Fine. Norwood, NJ: Ablex, 1988.

Woll, Bencie, Rachel Sutton-Spence, and Frances Elton. "Multilingualism: The Global Approach to Sign Languages." In *The Sociolinguistics of Sign Languages*, ed. Ceil Lucas, 8–32. Cambridge: Cambridge University Press, 2001

World Map

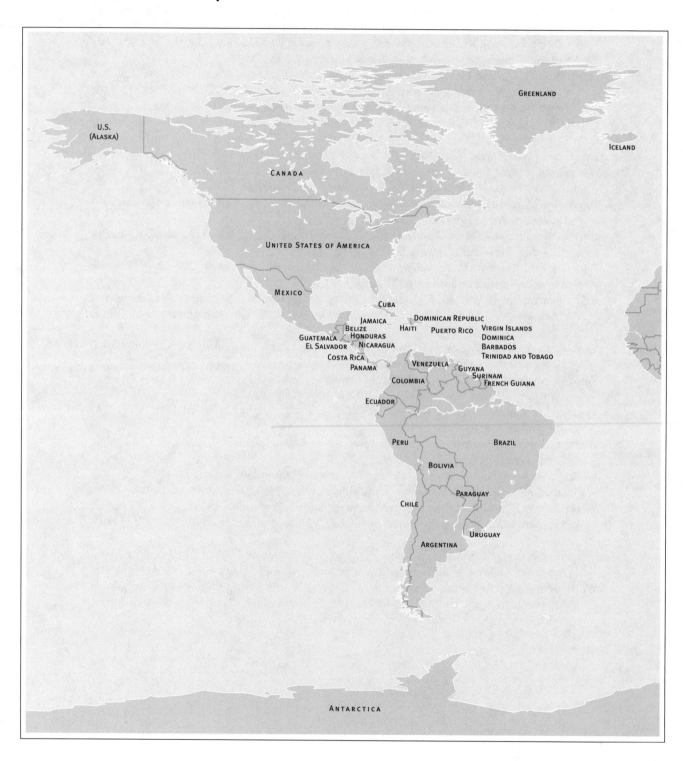

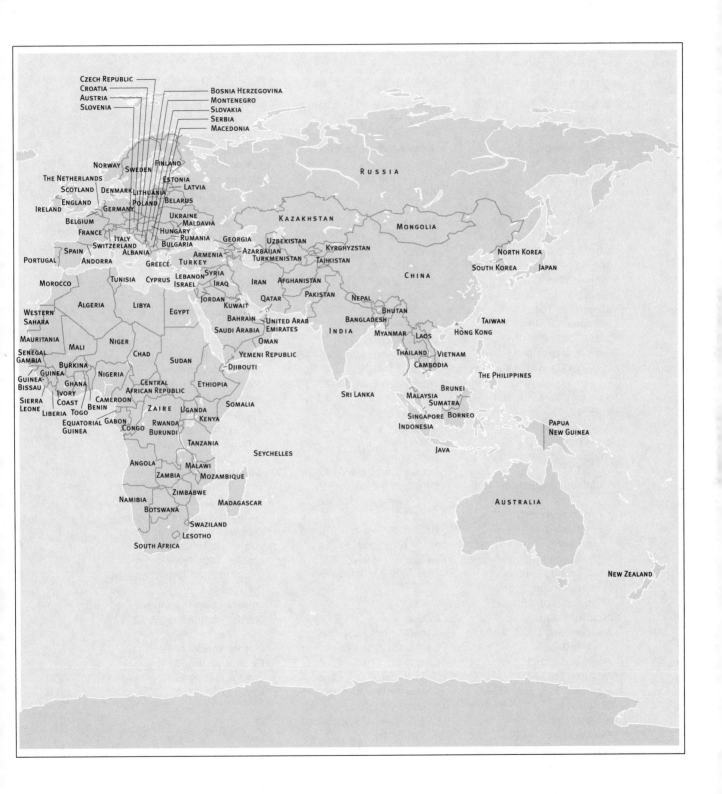

Index